Simon Mercieca

The Knights of St John in Malta

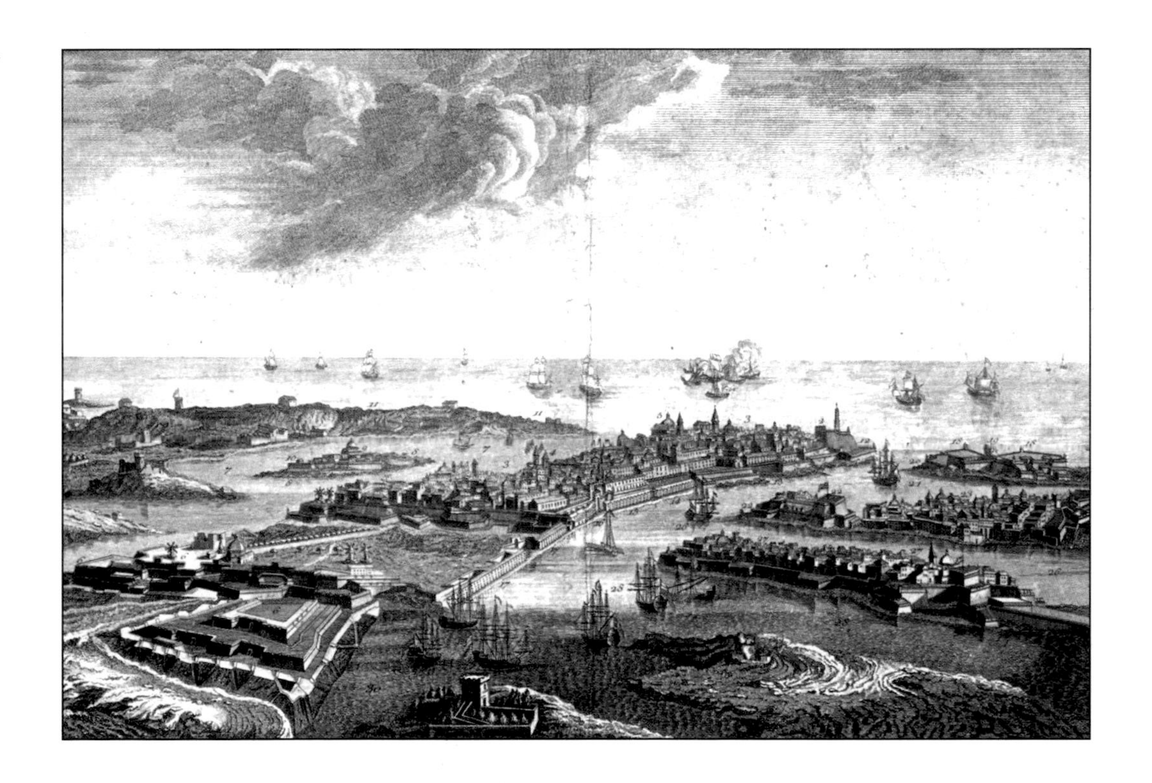

Miller Ditributors Limited - Miller House, Airport Way, Tarxien Road, Luqa LQA 05 Malta - P. O. Box 25, Malta International Airport LQA 05, Malta
Telephone: (356) 21 66 44 88 - Telefax: (356) 21 67 67 99 - E-mail: info@millermalta.com

To the Memory of
Edward DeGabriele

CONTENTS

Simon Mercieca currently occupies the post of Director of the Mediterranean Institute at the University of Malta. He is also a researcher on historical demography within the History Department and lectures on historical demographic subjects at the same University. In 1990 he graduated B.A. in History and Maltese and a year later obtained his B.A. (Hons.) degree in History. He furthered his studies in History at Master's level. During this period of study, he was awarded a scholarship by the *Istituto di Cultura Italiana* to study at the University of Rome *La Sapienza*. After he finished his Master's degree, he was awarded another scholarship to study historical demography at the University of Paris - Sorbonne. In 1995 he completed the *Diplôme d'Etude Approfondi* obtaining a Distinction. In 1998 he was invited by the University of the European Union at Florence to follow courses in historical demography. In 2002, Mr. Mercieca defended his thesis at the University of Paris – Sorbonne, entitled *Community Life in the Central Mediterranean: A Socio-Demographic Study of the Maltese Harbour Towns, Bormla 1586-1815*, and obtained his doctorate *cum laude*. Dr Mercieca has been invited to attend seminars and conferences in Greece, Israel, Morocco, Paris, Malta, Florence, Venice, Valencia, Cartagena, Pise, Tunis, Cagliari, Villefranche-sur-mer, Israel, Algiers and Egypt. He has also published a number of academic papers both in Malta and abroad.

Preface

The aim of this publication is to provide the reader with an overview of the deep historical associations between the island of Malta and the Order of Saint John. It particularly looks at the events that led up to the Order's arrival in Malta in 1530 and dwells on the celebrated Great Siege of 1565, when the Order and the Maltese withstood a four-month siege by the forces of the Ottoman Sultan, Suleiman II. The subsequent history of the Knights of St John and their control over the island, up to the date of the Order's expulsion from Malta by Napoleon Bonaparte in 1798, are also reviewed.

Indeed, if one had to apply the medieval approach to the writing of books, based on a *protocollum* (introductory part), a *contextus* (main text) and an *escatocollum* (concluding part) to the present publication, it could be said that this book has as its main text an account of the Great Siege, with a relation of the events relating to the foundation of the Order of Saint John as its *protocollum* and the overview of post-siege events serving as its *escatocollum*.

It should be stated at the outset that the historical record chronicling the Order's stay in Malta varies in detail, coverage and reliability. For instance, the story of the Great Siege of 1565, about which numerous accounts have been written, was largely based until recently on two major contemporary chronicles. The first was written by Giacomo Bosio, who was then the official historian of the Order of Saint John. Bosio had not been involved in the siege and therefore could not claim to having been an eyewitness, but he did have the advantage of being able to rely on first-hand information provided by figures within the Order and others who had been among the ranks of the besieged. Bosio produced a detailed and successful chronicle, structuring it in diary form in such a way that later historians were provided with a day-by-day account of the siege. This text, which he incorporated in the third volume of his *Sacra Historia* (Rome, 1602), remains an indispensable source for scholars of the history of Malta in the early decades of the Order's rule, especially because it is so entrenched in documentary evidence from the period and in other contemporary accounts that are now irretrievable.

LA VERDADERA RE
LACION DE TODO LO
q̃ eſte año de M.D.LXV. ha ſucedido en la
Iſla de Malta, dende antes que la armada del gran turco
Soliman llegaſſe ſobre ella, haſta la llegada del ſo-
corro poſtrero del poderoſiſsimo y catholico
Rey de Eſpaña don Phelipe nueſtro ſe-
ñor ſegũdo deſte nombre.

Recogida por Franciſco Balbi de Correggio en todo el ſitio Soldado.

Dirigida al Excellentiſsimo Don Iuan de Auſtria.

CON LICENCIA.

Impreſſa en Alcala de Henares en caſa de Iuan de Villanueva. Año 1567.

Francesco Balbi de Correggio's book on the Siege of Malta of 1565. National Library, Valletta.

The second major contemporary account was written by a Spanish mercenary, Francesco Balbi da Correggio, who during the siege was stationed at Fort Saint Michael in Senglea. Balbi da Correggio, like Bosio, came up with a day-by-day account of the siege which he later published in the form of a book (*La Verdadera Relacion de todo que este ano de MDLXV ha sucedido en la Isla de Malta*, Alcala de Henares, 1567). It appears that Balbi da Correggio enlisted as an arquebusier for the Order at the age of sixty – a course of action that was doubtless compelled by poverty and which is in keeping with the later description of him by Sir Harry Luke, a British military governor serving in Malta, as a 'luckless rolling stone'(Balbi, 5).

Bosio's and Balbi da Correggio's accounts shaped most subsequent writings about the siege, but the publication of a number of important studies in recent years has substantially enhanced historiography on the siege. Two books on the subject that are based on previously unpublished or otherwise little known documents should be mentioned here. The book

The frontispiece to the third volume of Bosio's Istoria. National Library, Valletta.

The 1565 Ottoman Malta Campaign Register (ed. A. Cassola, Malta 1998) reproduces the campaign register of the siege. The register was kept by the Turkish army in order to help determine the grants of land units to its soldiers as a reward for acts of bravery in combat. This practice, known within the Ottoman military as the *timar*, was an established form of compensation for participation in the war effort. Meanwhile, *A Study in Depth of 143 Maps Representing the Great Siege of Malta of 1565*, compiled by A. Ganado and M. Agius-Vadala (Malta, 1995), reproduces 143 maps relating to the siege which were published in Europe in commemoration and celebration of a significant triumph over the Ottoman Empire. It demonstrates that at the time there already existed ample and sophisticated recognition of the role of printing in the boosting of military morale and the development of an appropriate hagiography. The maps were in fact intended not only to disseminate news of the siege, but also to arouse popular appreciation of the achievement of the island's defenders.

The literature on the siege has continued to be enhanced by the recent republication of a rare sixteenth-century abstract on the siege, written by a Hospitaller knight, Fra Vincenzo Anastagi, who was stationed at Mdina during those turbulent days of battle. (G. Bonello, 'An Overlooked Eyewitness's Account of the Great Siege', *Melitensium Amor Festschrift in honour of Dun Gwann*, ed. T. Cortis, T. Freller, L. Bugeja, Malta, 2002). In addition, recent research on the stay of the Knights of Saint John in Malta has offered new grounds for the revaluation of Malta's past during this period. Worthy of mention here are the essays in *Hospitaller Malta* edited by Professor V. Mallia Milanes (Malta, 1993) and Joseph F. Grima's modern and comprehensive rereading of the Hospitaller's history in his book, written in Maltese, entitled *Zmien il-Kavalieri f'Malta 1530-1798* (Malta, 2001). These studies and others specified in the bibliography provided the basis for the research that led to this book's compilation. I have also brought to bear my own research in a number of archives relating to the history of the Order's rule in Malta.

I should like to record here my gratitude for the outstanding help I received during the writing of this book. This work would not have gone to press by the deadlines required had it not been for the assistance of my friend and colleague, Dr. Ivan Callus. I am also very grateful to Mr. Malcolm Miller, for his faith in the project and his support of my research, and for commissioning me with the writing of this publication.

Finally, I should like to state that this work is dedicated to the memory of a friend of mine, Dr. Edward DeGabriele.

Prelude

At the end of his diplomatic mission in 1667, the Inquisitor and Papal legate to Malta, Monsignor Angelo Ranuzzi (1667-1668), wrote to his superiors in Rome about general conditions on the island. In conformity with Venetian diplomatic praxis at the time, European ambassadors had begun to compile at the end of their mission a concise description of the country in which they were assigned service. Ranuzzi opened his *Relatione* (as this diplomatic document was called) with a succinct description of what Malta had come to represent under the Knights of St John. "Your Holiness," Ranuzzi wrote, "Malta is an island at the extreme end of Christianity." The statement is significant because, pronounced exactly at the mid-term of the Knights' tenure of Malta, it is symptomatic of contemporary perceptions of the island within the highest levels of European diplomacy. While Malta was not in fact the farthest point of Christianity (by 1667, Christianity had the firmest of roots in the New World), it was still being regarded as an eminently strategic bulwark against Ottoman expansionism.

The island's sensitive location in the middle of the Mediterranean explains in part why it became an island fostering, after 1530, a sense of nostalgia for the medieval notions of chivalry. It was ideally placed for any aristocratic order committed to a military mission in the defence of Christendom. Set on the fringes of the Latin West, it could serve as the ideal springboard for the harassment of the Ottoman Turks. This *frontiera barbarorum* was transformed by the Knights of Saint John into one of the most

Coat of Arms of Inquisitors, at their Palace in Birgu.

Aerial view of Valletta.

The Auberge used by the knights of Provence in Birgu. Each Langue housed its Knights in a separate Auberge or Convent.

impregnable European bulwarks against the enemies of the Christian faith. It became a thorn in the side of the Ottoman Turks. In this dialectic of war between Islam and Christianity, between Barbary and Hospitaller corsairs, Malta would also become a point of contact between the Muslim East and the Christian West. This religious confrontation brought to the island a number of Muslim slaves whose skin colour varied from white to black, while travellers on their way to or from the Levant often made a short stop in Malta. Indeed, people from varying cultures mingled in the streets of Valletta, the new capital city of Malta, from 1566.

A realistic rather than nostalgic viewpoint, however, must emphasise that the sixteenth and seventeenth centuries were not easy times. The French historian, Fernand Braudel, described small Mediterranean islands as lands of hunger: isolated worlds. It is an evaluation made in the light of the awareness of post-medieval realities of time and space. Inefficient transportation intensified the barrier of distance and the natural insularity imposed by the surrounding sea. The hilly and indifferently surfaced terrain was mostly traversed on foot. Horses were somewhat rare, and donkeys were the preferred beast of burden: they might have been slower, but were more suited to the inland surroundings of Malta.

Adverse environmental conditions, especially on those islands where cultivable land was limited, further penalised human existence. For those islands that were not self-sufficient, shipping was crucial in guaranteeing

the provision of basic necessities.
Malta was a case in point. Throughout the late medieval period, agricultural production could not meet the demands of a population of about fifteen thousand people. The local medieval government, popularly known as the *Universitas,* had had to rely on the importation of grain from Sicily, and arrangements were made to bring over wheat and other cereals at a subsidised price.

It was such difficulties that the Knights of St John would come to both know and mitigate. Their stay on the island was one of the most far-reaching occupations in Malta's long history as a land of conquest for successive powers. Under their rule, Malta would become less of an isolated world, both economically and politically, and would take on an increasingly pivotal role in the balance of power as this played itself out in the Mediterranean basin. At the same time that this was happening, the Knights were creating infrastructures that are still prominent up to this day.
Their contribution to the architectural fabric of the country and their construction of new urban centres, palaces, auberges and churches is hard to overlook. It is not too surprising then that Malta, once seen by the Knights themselves as an extreme outpost of Christianity, is sometimes seen in our days as an outpost of knighthood nostalgia: a site where all those who look with reverential awe upon the achievements and tribulations of the great military orders of Europe's past can come to retrace some of the most significant episodes in the history of what must rank as among the most prominent of the chivalric Orders.

Detail from the staircase of the Auberge of the Knights of Provence in Birgu.

The Origins of the Knights of St John

Chapter 1

The origins of the Knights of Saint John are unclear, and are shrouded in the uncertainties of history. There are two main accounts of how they came into being. The first posits an Italian origin, ascribing it to links with merchants from the Italian city of Amalfi, who in those distant days were actively trading in the Levant. This theory has entered mainstream chronicles of the Knights' history. The second is more Francophile, and links the Knights' origins to the travels of French pilgrims to the Holy Lands. Whichever of these theories is true, the Knights' origins are to be linked to a particular moment in European history: the resurgence of the Latin West as a Mediterranean power. Gradually, Europe, in particular realms in France and Spain, found the strength and means to counter the Arab expansion of the sixth century, which over a span of five hundred years had led to an Empire that extended from Baghdad to Spain. In the eleventh century, European powers gained the confidence to replace a policy of protracted defensiveness with a greater disposition for attack. They were to take advantage of internal division within the Muslim world, where the Abassyd monarchy of Spain was at war with the Fatimids' kingdom of Egypt. Between two antagonists, an Italian saying goes, the third party wins. In this situation, the third party was predominantly constituted by the Latin West. In particular, the emerging Normans were seeking new lands. They cast their attention on Jerusalem and the surrounding territories, and took the battle there, taking advantage of friction in the area known today as the Middle East between the Seldjuk Turks and the Fatimids of Egypt. The time was ripe for any power wanting to affirm its hold on the area to step in. On its part, the Byzantine Empire from its base in Constantinople could not offer hard resistance to the rising power of the Seldjuk, in whose hands it lost the control of Jerusalem. With Byzantium in a long process of decline, it was only the West, through the impetus derived from the formation of a strong Latin Church, that could finally react to the rapid expansion of Islam. The success of Islam was partly attributed by the West to the way in which its armies were raised. Soon, Christian forces would be devising recruitment methods emulating the spirit of the Islamic Jihad. The participants in these 'holy wars' on the Christian side, as they were referred to in the West, began to be known as Crusaders; one of the reasons being that they carried the symbol of the cross on their surcoat, emphasising that the conflict was ostensibly about religion. In theory, the Crusades, sanctioned by the rhetoric of Holy Wars, were initially intended to secure the expulsion of Muslims from the lands held sacred by Christians having been inhabited by Jesus Christ. Many in Europe believed in this appeal. But in practice, the holy wars degenerated, like most wars, into battles for the conquest of new living space.

A lead seal showing an Oriental city on the Eastern shores of the Mediterranean as it appeared in the eyes of Western crusaders. National Library, Valletta.

The First Crusade, called by Pope Urban II in 1095, showed that if the Christian forces wanted to keep hold of their conquests, victories had to be followed by the consolidation of power. The Christian powers, in particular French barons and the Pope, recognised the importance of permanent garrisons in the East, not only for purposes of defence but also to offer shelter and succour to the many pilgrims that flocked to the Holy Land. In the event, the Crusaders proved themselves to be more formidable in attack than in defence. They succeeded in occupying vast territories in a relatively short period of time, as in the space of four years they had most of Palestine, including Jerusalem, in their hands. However, they encountered great difficulties when it came to securing their hold over the conquered lands. Their cause was not helped by the logistical problems created by the fact that the mass gathering of such a huge crusading army depended on the issuing of the crusading bull, which was the Pope's sole prerogative. Technically, Papal approval was required for a crusading mission. Subjecting a military organisation to Papal whim was rather impractical for the particular circumstances appertaining to the Holy Land. The setting up of the Latin kingdom of Outremer in 1099, as the conquered territories in the east were called, was hampered by a military logic that was constrained by the rule of subservience to Rome or Avignon. On its part, the papacy envisaged military action as something to be carried out under its exclusive auspices. This enhanced the power of Rome. A compromise was to some extent achieved with the elevation of a number of Knights' congregations, (which had sprouted in Palestine to defend Christian pilgrims in the Holy Land) to religious orders with a military task.

It was against this backdrop that the Order of St John became an approved Order of the Church in 1113. It was not the sole organization in Palestine to be elevated into a regular order of the Church. The Templars and the Teutonic Knights were two other institutions which received this privilege, both becoming monks with military duties and acquiring a constitution that procured them political power and extensive influence over the European noble families from which they recruited their members.

The establishment of the Knights of Saint John into a regular order of the Church came at a time when the *res publica Cristiana* (as the Christian commonwealth was called at the time) was already split between East and West, in the form of the division between Orthodox and Latin Christians. The Hospitallers' ranks reflected this split, as recruitment was open only to Latin Christians. In addition, the institution developed an internal hierarchy, where rank was associated with different grades of power and functions. Indeed, by the thirteenth century three principal tiers of Hospitallers were in existence: the Knights, the Chaplains and the Servants-at-Arms.

An eighteenth-century representation by the French painter Antoine Favray of the acclaimed founder of the Hospitaller Order, the Blessed Gerard, attending the sick in a xenodocium in Jerusalem. Museum of Fine Arts, Valletta.

At first, the Order's mission focused on the care of the sick and the offering of shelter to pilgrims to the Holy Land. However, rising tensions in the East, discord between Christians themselves, and wars against Islam highlighted the need for the physical defence of the faith on the conquered territories. Slowly, the latter became the primary aim of the military Orders. In the Order of Saint John, this responsibility fell primarily to the professed Knights. They were the warring brethren sanctioned to use force to protect the Latin interest in the East. This could be the reason why these brothers became the most respected branch of all the Hospitaller institution. Every aspect of the Order began to revolve around these brethren. The most prestigious ranks and functions were reserved for these Knights. The Master of the Order was to be elected from within their restricted circle.
The Chaplains were at first entrusted with tending to the spiritual needs of the sick, but by the thirteenth century they are encountered performing the

The Bull of Pascal II issued in 1113 making the Hospitallers an approved Order of the Church. National Library, Valletta.

spiritual duties and rituals expected from a religious order, such as the saying of the mass and the liturgical offices. The Servants-at-Arms were a supportive group created to assist the Knights in their military duties. These internal tiers soon assumed distinctions based on social class. The rank of Knight became the exclusive preserve of the nobility, whilst the other grades were left open to those of bourgeois ancestry. The Chaplains began to be divided between the Conventual Chaplains, or those assigned to the religious duties in the Convent, and the Magistral Chaplains, who performed their duties in the Hospitallers' priories – or convents – that the Order held all over Europe. Practically in all the major European cities, as in Paris, Messina, Venice, Rome, Barletta, Prague and Aix-in-Provence, to mention just a few cases, the Order of Saint John opened a convent to serve as residence for the Knights and from which they administered a number of land units, called commanderies.

The Knights' constitution, particularly the contradiction by which a religious Order whose original ethos was charitable could take on an increasingly militaristic role, must be read in terms of the socio-political circumstances of the time. Technically, monks were debarred from taking part in armed struggle, as canonical impositions on the clergy disallowed participation in such an activity. This reflected a centuries-old custom, with roots in both Judaic and Greek traditions, whereby priests could not stain their anointed hands with blood. Yet the bull issued by Pope Paschal II in 1113, by which the Knights of Saint John were established as a religious order, sought to reconcile two different ethics in giving rise to an oxymoronic category of warrior monks. The constitution adopted was in fact religious in inspiration. Those seeking admittance to the Order were to take the vows of chastity, obedience and poverty, and to follow the Augustinian rule. This was a nicely calculated stratagem, aimed at avoiding interference from any Christian state or bishopric, for as members of a religious order of the Church, the brethren owed their loyality to their Master who then owed direct allegiance to the Pope. Yet, this constitution allowed latitude for a militaristic vocation by sanctioning the establishment of an arm within the Order that was devoted solely to war. The 'Knights of Justice and Obedience', as those knights taking up a military mission came to be known, took the religious vows but were not allowed to celebrate Mass. In other words, the Knights' constitution was deliberately formulated to supply the papacy with a canonical loophole for the establishment of a class of 'warrior monks'. As it turned out, these would gradually acquire greater prestige than those brothers dedicated to divine service.

The recruitment of Knights from different areas of Western Europe would lead to the formation of seven *Langues*, whose number was increased to eight in the fifteenth century. These Langues were constituted to reflect the division of power in Europe across diverse kingdoms, in accordance with different languages spoken in different parts of Western Europe in the thirteenth century. It was on the basis of this linguistic difference that they were called Langues, a Romance word whose closest equivalent is the English word *Tongue*. In effect, the Langues reflected medieval geopolitical realities that, by the time the Order came to Malta, had already been supplanted. Knights hailing from France were divided into three Langues: those from the Languedoc were assigned to the Langue of Provence, those from the Languedoil to France, and the Bretons to Auvergne.

An idealised image of a Hospitaller nun looking after female pilgrims or destitute women. Wignacourt Museum, Rabat.

A seventeenth-century painting having in the foreground the image of the first Master of the Hospitaller Order, the French Raymond Du Puy (1120-1160). In the background, Hospitaller Knights and other crusaders fight the infidels for the control of the Holy Land. Wignacourt Musuem, Rabat.

Spanish Knights were assigned to one Langue until the fifteenth century, but this was later split between Castile (which incorporated also Portugal) and Aragon (which had Catalonia and Navarre). Italy, Germany (the latter included Scandinavia and Bohemia-Poland) and England (with Ireland) were each assigned one Langue. This kind of internal division was by no means extraordinary, and it has to be regarded as an elaboration of already established practices observed by major medieval monastic institutions. These often structured themselves in a way which reflected boundaries between medieval national territories while referring supervision and control to a Superior-General, or Master.
The head of each Langue, who was known in the Hospitallers' jargon as Pilier, came to assume an important office in the Order's governance. Provence was given the privilege of providing the Grand Commander, responsible for control and administration of the Hospitallers' property. Auvergne provided the Marshal, a senior military officer responsible for overseeing the land forces. France held the post of the Hospitaller, which held the overall responsibility for the running of the Knights' hospital. Italy was assigned the post of the Admiralty, while to Spain went the Drapier, a sort of quartermaster general under whose care fell the overall responsibility for the Hospital's supplies. England assumed the responsibility for the Turcopolier, a military post in charge of the cavalry and Germany oversaw the Grand Bailiff, or the office responsible for the audit of the administration of the Hospitallers' land.

The Templars and the Hospitallers

Chapter 2

As already suggested above, the military importance assumed by the Knights of Saint John from the twelfth century onwards represented a deviation from its founding ethos. The military orders trace their origins to the work of nursing monks managing hospices, or *xenodochia,* in both Palestine and Europe. These offered spiritual care and medical attention to pilgrims. As the Greek word *xenodochia* clearly indicates, their objective was to receive foreigners (*xeno*) in their hostelries (*dochia*). Their evolution into warrior monks arose from the pressure brought to bear from the realities of conditions encountered by Christians in the East, in particular the continuous need for armed resistance to the Seldjuk first, the Mamelukes later, and ultimately the Ottoman Turks.

The loss of the Holy Land to the Seldjuk Turks threw the military orders into a profound crisis. Their *raison d'être*, linked to the ethic of *defensio fidei*, appeared to lose both gloss and relevance. The strongest military Order, the *Milites Templi Hierosolimitani* (or, in more popular idiom, the Templars), was the worst affected. Hindsight shows (as will be detailed below) that the fourteenth-century decision taken by the Knights of Saint John to remain in the East – an option viewed at the time as one that was stubbornly foolhardy – spared them suppression and persecution later. In the event, the Templars moved to Cyprus and then France, while the Teutonics settled in Eastern Prussia. On their part, the Knights of Saint John embarked on the occupation of Crete. Soon, however, they would abandon the project in favour of joining the Templars and establishing their headquarters on the Latin Kingdom of Cyprus. The Hospitallers' sojourn in Cyprus was short. The Latin king of Cyprus, Henry II, was against the settlement of equestrian Orders in his realm and did his utmost to drive both the Templars and the Hospitallers out. The Templars retired to France while the Hospitallers sought a new home in the region, and by 1306 they were successfully establishing themselves on the island of Rhodes. It was this development that partly accounts for their avoidance of the same fate befalling the Templars. It was also the first time that the Knights of Saint John would feel nostalgic for the time spent in the Holy Land. Rhodes was in part conquered to fulfil the Knights' wish to have a stronghold at a short distance from the lost holy places. Rhodes' geographical position could ideally serve as a port of call for the Christian pilgrims on their route to Jerusalem, whilst its proximity to Palestine turned it into an ideal stepping-stone for the liberation of these sacred places from Muslim control.

Stylised image of a medieval monarch. Philip the Fair of France is often represented in this posture. National Library, Valletta.

The annihilation of the Templars is perhaps the best known episode in the history of military monastic institutions – apart from the Great Siege of Malta of 1565. The most common reason given for the execution of the Templars at the stake was the rapacity of the French King, Philip the Fair, who at the turn of the thirteenth century was anxious to acquire their property. In reality, the circumstances were somewhat more complex. The French King could avail himself only of the movable property of the Templars, as the immovable property was bequeathed by Pope Clement V to the Knights of Saint John and consequently provided the lion's share of the Hospitallers' revenues.

A possible representation, on a lead seal, of the gates of the city of Jerusalem. National Library, Valletta.

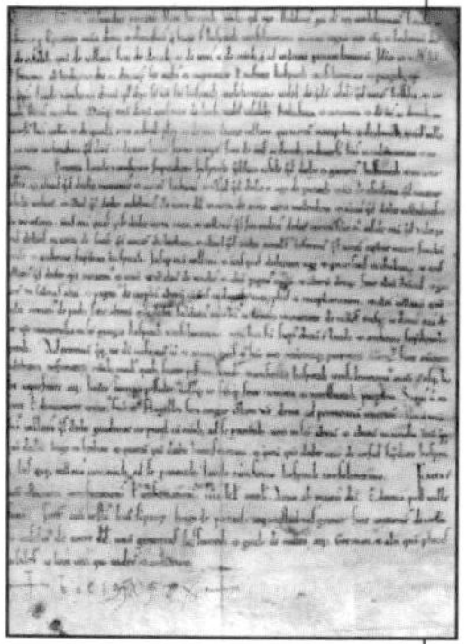

King Baldwin's donation of land to the Hospital Order in Palestine at the time of the crusades. National Library, Valletta.

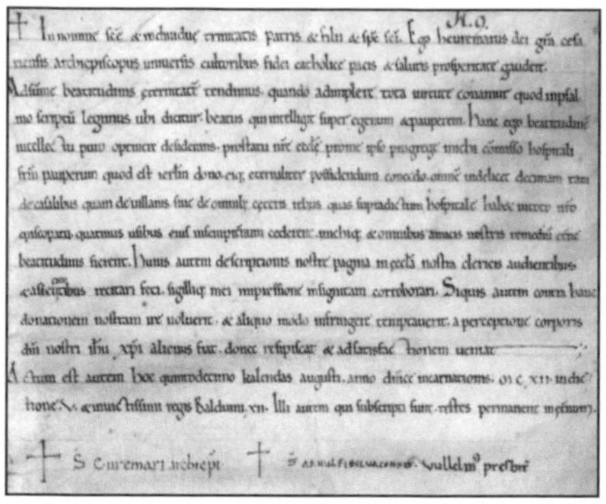

An original **pergamena** ***of land donations by an ecclesiastical institution to the Hospitaller Order of Malta. National Library, Valletta.***

Part of the seal that was attached to a **pergamena** ***of land donations. National Library, Valletta.***

To understand the background to this, reference has to be made to the fact that fundamental to the formation of the monastic orders were the bequests of commanderies, or 'land units'. The archives of the Order at Valletta still house a collection of *pergamena*, dating back to the twelfth century, which are a testimony to this practice; some originals have still their lead seal attached, while others are medieval copies of original acts of donations of lands situated both in the Middle East and Europe. The military orders' consequent evolution as staggeringly powerful and wealthy landowners goes a long way towards explaining why for a long time they were so well regarded within the European nobility, especially in Italy and France.

In Europe the military orders, particularly the Hopitallers, the Templars, the Order of Saint Lazarus, the Holy Sepulchre and the Teutonics, sought to link their hospitality closely to their military activity in the Holy Land. *Hospitia* or *xenodochia* began to emerge at strategic points on the principal routes of communications that connected Italy with other countries, like France, or that crossed the country from the Alps to Messina, leading either to Italy's main harbour cities or to Rome. At the *hospitium*, travellers, especially pilgrims, not only found physical comfort but also spiritual assistance, as these hospices were often endowed with an adjacent chapel.

The Hospitallers' concentration on the pilgrims' routes leading to Rome could possibly explain why their institution was less popular, in terms of donations from pilgrims, than other Orders. Their rivals or competitors, the Templars, possessed much more extensive properties in Europe, and they were often preferred in wills, legacies and endowments. In addition, the Templars' concentration on the *viae* which radiated to ports of embarkation doubtlessly lent them greater exposure with pilgrims and land seekers heading for Palestine. It must be remembered that Jerusalem remained, until the late thirteenth century, the preferred destination for Christian pilgrims. The strong concentration of hospices administered by the Templars on the way to Jerusalem contributed to making their Order one of the most popular with pilgrims, and helped the attraction of significant bequests. In consequence, by the thirteenth century the Templars wielded formidable economic and political force. This led not only to the forging of significant alliances but also to the contracting of enmities and trouble with the authorities in certain territories, so that the safeguarding of their autonomy became an increasingly fraught enterprise.

The debacle in the Crusades, and the fall of the last Christian bulwark at Acre in 1291, would come to be a momentous turning point. The fall of Acre forced the Hospitallers and the Teutonic Knights to diversify their operations and review their ethic. Whereas the Hospitallers did this by attempting the conquest of Rhodes, the Teutonics chose to concentrate on the defence of the German borders against heathen forces. The Templars' return to Europe, and the dissipation of their activities into little more than wardenship of their estates in France, was ill-considered. As they became too strong and too independent a force for the French realm to contend with, their inertia in terms of their former objectives and dynamism prompted criticism in many quarters and antagonism in others. The historical validity of the malicious gossip that surrounds the Templars' supposed licentious behaviour is currently being revaluated by the historian Jonathan Riley-Smith, who believes that the rumours and accusations were well founded. Such dissolute behaviour did them no favours either.

Meanwhile the Hospitallers were concentrating on the *Viae Romae*, with the consequence that their mansions began to acquire exceptional value, especially as Rome was now being regarded as the second Jerusalem. In contrast, the Templars' hospitality structures were beginning to lose much of their value. Their hospice network ended up on the periphery of emerging destinations for pilgrimages, tarnishing the Order's reputation. Their militarism was overshadowing their hospitaller activity, and accusations of licentiousness would set the scene for their indictment. On 12 August 1308, Clement V issued *Faciens Misericordiam*, a bull nominating a commission to investigate the crimes of which the Templars were being accused. It proved to be a difficult assignment, especially as Papal Inquisitors reached contrasting opinions; some sought to defend or protect the Templars, others were overzealous in their prosecution. The city of Tortona provides an interesting example of this conflict. Between 1308 and 1312, the Inquisitor there was threatened at various stages of his investigation by the nobles for daring to undertake criminal procedures against the Templars. The impasse persuaded the Pope to issue another bull, *Alma mater ecclesia*, on 4 September 1310. The inquiring magistrates were exhorted to conclude, in the shortest time possible, their investigations against the Templars and to submit their compilation of evidence to the city of Avignon in France, which at the time was hosting the Papal residence. Other bulls, with similar exhortations, followed, until on 3 April 1312 Clement V bowed to the pressure exerted by Philip the Fair and published, during the course of the Council of Vienna, the bull *Vox (Clamantis) in Excelso,* suppressing the Templars. The bull seems to have been designed as a compromise placating the opposing factions. The Templars were not excommunicated outright; instead, they were forbidden to operate within the framework of the Catholic Church. Philip the Fair's hopes of acquiring through Papal dispensation the rich lands of the Templars in France were frustrated. In a month's time, on 6 May, a second bull, *Ad Providam*, was issued. The Pope allotted all the property of the Templars to the Order of St John, with the exception of their estates in Aragon, Castile, Portugal and Majorca.

Thus, the concentration of the Hospitaller Order on the *Viae Romae,* the network of roads that led to Rome, as well as their commitment to their engagement in the East with the conquest of Rhodes, may have contributed towards preventing them from meeting the fate of the Templars, and indeed of rendering them worthy recipients of the Templars' property. The fact that

A portrait of the thirteenth-century Hospitaller nun, Ubaldesca, who dedicated her life to the care of pilgrims. Wignacourt Museum, Rabat.

Figures of a Teutonic, a Hospitaller and a Templar Knight. Inquisitor's Palace, Birgu.

lands and from secular powers aspiring to them. The process took decades to complete, and in the fifteenth century the Order was still in the process of receiving property from the Templars. The inheritance of the Templars' property also perpetuated already existing confusions over the identities of the Templars and the Hospitallers. The similarity in names did not help: *templum sive domum Millicie Templi Hierosolimitani,* or *Templari,* for short, designated the former, while the latter were called *Templari Sancti Johannis*. The passing of the Templars' property increased the confusion in the identification of these two Orders, because some of the acquired lands continued to be called *del Tempio*, while others continued to retain the Templars' original name, undergoing slight variations or having their original appellation extended by the addition of the Latin genitive form of the word *Sancti Johannis* in direct reference to the Hospitallers' patron saint.

the Hospitaller Order had a significant constituency of French knights may also have played a determining role in their being preferred over other Orders like the Teutonic, whose acquisition of such lands might otherwise have affected the balance of political power in Europe.

Nonetheless, the Order of St John's appropriation of the Templars' property was an enterprise that carried considerable financial and political complications, as well as one which attracted strong resistance from some quarters, in particular from those who were occupying these

Painting of Saint John the Baptist, the Hospitallers' patron saint, with Saint Paul by the Antoine Favray. Wignacourt Museum, Rabat.

A Garden of Eden called Rhodes

Chapter 3

The occupation of the island of Rhodes necessitated an unavoidable change in the internal structure of the Order of Saint John. In Outremer, the Hospitallers depended primarily on land armies for their defence. In Rhodes, the Hospitallers had to pursue new ventures in the maritime field. The *Militia Christi* would soon diversify its focus from that concentrated on a land force to one envisaging strong naval operations. It was as a result of the putting together of a small fleet during the Order's short sojourn in Cyprus (1292-1306) that Master Foulques de Villaret was later able to sail to Rhodes around 1306 and, with two galleys and 35 knights and 500 infantrymen, conquer the capital, Philermos. This event impacted negatively on the concept of a Christian commonwealth, and its repercussions continued to reverberate upon the Hospitaller institution for centuries to come, as the Order had gone against its principles and constitution in attacking a territory held by Christians. Its ethos was bound up with the struggle against Islamic power and not with attacks on Greek Orthodox Christians.

However, the island of Rhodes represented the recovery of a forsaken principle. The last decades of the Hospitallers' stay in Outremer had forced the Order to abandon its hospitality mission. Rhodes gave them the opportunity to recover this lost ideal by once again making it possible to open a *xenodochia* to receive distressed pilgrims.

It should also be noted that it was in Rhodes that the naval mission of the Knights was consolidated. The Knights adapted the medieval feudal system to their naval needs. In Rhodes, the peasants were subjected to serfdom which was now adopted in such a way that instead of tying the male labour force to the fields, many were compelled to participate in what came to be known as *servitudo marina*. Generation after generation had some of its male members conscripted to work on the Hospitallers' vessels, helping to make the Order's naval strength formidable. Indeed, the Hospitallers were invited by the Christian forces in the East, in particular by the Kingdom of Cyprus, to organise raids on Mameluke Egypt.

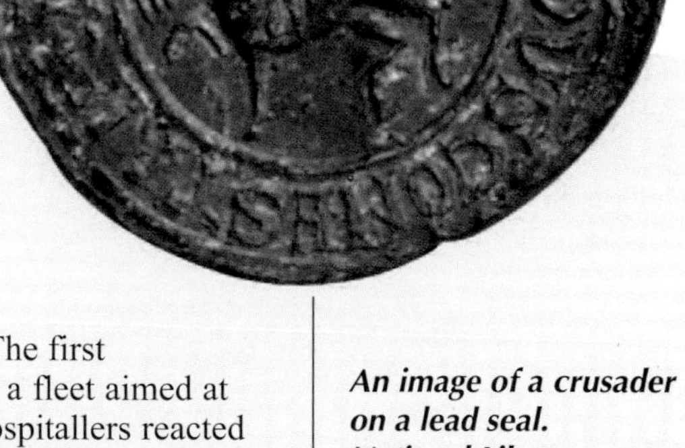

An image of a crusader on a lead seal. National Library, Valletta.

The island of Rhodes came to represent a Garden of Eden for the Knights. Its fertile plains and mild climate made it something of an earthly paradise. Besides the abundance of water – a rare commodity in the Braudelian 'isolated worlds' of the Mediterranean – the island was rich in orange and lemon groves, yielding two fruits that were at the time exotic and rare delicacies in northwestern Europe.

Yet, the Hospitallers' tenancy of Rhodes would soon be challenged. The first significant attack was mounted in 1440. Sultan Jakmak of Egypt sent a fleet aimed at halting the Order's corsairing attacks on Egyptian commerce. The Hospitallers reacted by having their Marshal, Fra Louis de Saint Sebastien, gather a fleet and counter-attacking. Heavy losses were inflicted on the Mameluke forces, but the vastness of their kingdom made any losses insignificant, Jakmak made another attempt in 1444. This time, an Egyptian force of 18,000 succeeded in disembarking on Rhodes and laying siege to the city, subjecting it to heavy bombardment and breaching its defences. Despite this initial setback, the Hospitallers received timely reinforcements from Burgundy and Catalonia. An army was gathered and the two sides met in the open field, with the Knights earning a decisive victory and forcing Jakmak to agree to peace terms in 1446.

The hero of the siege of Constantinople of 1453, Mehmet II, whose forces had conquered the last vestiges of Byzantine rule in the East, would be the next to put the strength of Rhodes to the test. The attack came in 1480. It was the inevitable reaction to

The Grandmaster Pierre d'Aubusson, who was the man who led the Knights to a successful victory over the Turks in 1480. National Library, Valletta.

the Knights' long disruption of Turkish shipping and consistent raiding of Anatolia (i.e. modern-day Turkey). Looking at the siege with the benefit of hindsight, the Turkish invasion can be seen as a somewhat belated attack. However, as Mehmet II was occupied with the pressures exerted by the crumbling Byzantine Empire, it was only after successfully besieging Constantinople in 1453 and thereafter subjecting Romania to his rule that his attention could turn to the island of the Knights. Foreseeing the danger of an attack, the Knights counterbalanced the anticipated Ottoman expedition by building a network of fortifications all around the city of Rhodes and by deepening the moats.

This defence system was of such a strength as to constrain Mehmet II to put an Ottoman attack on the island among his last priorities. The Turkish sultan had to wait twenty-seven years before he was in a position to despatch a massive force of around 70,000 men against Rhodes. What may have possibly been the most heavily fortified city of all Christendom was to endure a three-month siege.

The Turks landed in Rhodes on 22 May. The pattern that developed would be repeated in the siege of Malta of 1565. After heavy bombardment, the walls of Rhodes were breached. However, the Turks were prevented from advancing into the city by ferocious resistance, during which the Grandmaster Pierre d'Aubusson, was lightly wounded. The Christian garrison of Rhodes found the energy and resources to mount a counter-attack, breaching the enemy's camp and capturing the Turkish standard. But what finally persuaded the Turks to sound the retreat was the arrival in Rhodes of naval reinforcements, consisting of a Papal brigantine and a Neapolitan carrack carrying fresh troops, victuals and armaments much needed by the besieged.

The retreat of the Ottoman force conferred prestige and honour upon Grandmaster D'Aubusson, and in 1485 he was elevated to the rank of cardinal. In truth, however, the Ottomans had only lost the battle, not the war. The definitive loss of Rhodes would come about 42 years later. Until that siege in 1522, the Ottomans would experience internal political crisis as a result of Mehmet II's death. The Order showed considerable diplomatic skill in the conflict over succession between two of Mehmet's sons, Bayezid and Djem, by playing them off against each other. The internal fight was soon to end with the weaker, Djem, petitioning the Knights for political asylum. This was duly granted. However, as Djem was an awkward partner for the Knights, and as his stay in Rhodes could have endangered the security of the island, he was placed on a ship sailing to Europe under the protection of the French and Papal courts. Meanwhile, a house rebellion brought Bayezid's downfall for he was forced to abdicate in 1512. This tragic story did not end there. The Ottoman internal security still considered him a threat and he was eventually assassinated by poison. His brother Djem met the same fate. Thus, Bayezid's successor, Selim I, popularly known as the Grim, was assured of having no internal competition to his claims over the throne.

Selim I sought to resurrect and consolidate the policies of his grandfather Mehmet II, and waged wars in central Europe, but his biggest success was in the Levant through the subjection of Persia in 1514, Syria in 1516 and Egypt in 1517. The conquest of Egypt signalled the end of the Mameluke dynasty. Its last king was beheaded, leaving the way clear for the house of Osman's (as the Ottoman dynasty was called) claims on religious hegemony over the Muslim world. Only his death in 1521 prevented Selim I from

A representation of a Turkish assault on a Hospitaller enclave. It probably represents the assault on Rhodes of 1522. Museum of Fine Arts, Valletta.

conquering Rhodes, which stood out as his most obvious objective. That task fell to his successor, his son Suleiman the Magnificent. In June 1522, Suleiman sent a flotilla of 103 galleys and 300 other vessels against Rhodes.

Two of the protagonists who took part in the siege of Rhodes of 1522 would figure heavily in the siege of Malta of 1565. The first was Suleiman the Magnificent himself. The second was the commander-in-chief of the land army, Mustapha Pasha, who at the time was still a young and inexperienced general. However, as Suleiman's brother-in-law he was guaranteed a high position in the army.

As with the battle of 1480, the siege opened with the attackers launching concentrated mortar fire against the city of Rhodes, which served as the Knights' main fort. As the Turks had rightly calculated, all the peripheral military structures would capitulate once the main stronghold fell into their hands. Thus, they spared their energies and refrained from attacking the Hospitallers fort at Bodrum in Asia Minor and the castle at Kasterlorizon.

The Knights put up a heroic resistance under Grandmaster Fra Philippe Villiers de L'Isle Adam, even if they were fighting what historians of the Order have later

Grandmaster Philippe Villiers de L'Isle Adam. National Library, Valletta.

described as a battle against impossible odds, for, unlike 1480, reinforcements failed to arrive. Venice was the only power at the time that could lend a hand. But Venice's only interest was to foster its good relations with the Porte (as the Ottomans were normally known in Europe at the time) rather than succouring the Order, which was perceived by the Venetians as a threat to their trade in the Levant. Thus, all Venetian ports in the East were closed to members of the Order who might have sought to gain a passage to Rhodes. Denied aid from Europe, the famine-stricken population began to be afflicted by disease.

Furthermore, the Turks had the advantage of fighting at a short distance from their home base. This was of paramount importance in sixteenth-century military logistics, as it guaranteed the flow of supplies, especially in the key winter season. In fact, as winter approached, Suleiman's forces had no problems in proceeding with the siege.

On the other hand, deprived of any assistance from the West, it was natural that after a siege which was approaching its six month, the Grandmaster Fra Philippe Villiers de L'Isle Adam would be compelled to seek a truce. Suleiman II, who had personally supervised the conflict by travelling to Rhodes, was disposed to grant the Knights an honourable surrender. The Hospitallers were granted the honours of arms, besides being allowed to leave Rhodes with their treasures, which included the icon of the Madonna of Philermos, the key of Rhodes, sacred vestments and, most importantly, their archives. They left on 1 January 1523, little knowing that they were embarking on an eight-year odyssey before they would find another home.

The loss of Rhodes pitched the Order's administration into crisis, and dealt a big blow to any vestigial nostalgia for the medieval ideals of chivalry that had been built up over the 200-year stay on this island.

Yet the Order, like the phoenix, was soon to rise from its ashes. As the events the sixteenth century have shown, its defeat was far from total. In less than eight years, the setback of Rhodes was overcome, whilst the combative spirit was rediscovered in less than 23 years. But until this latter event was to happen, the Hospitallers would undergo a process of self-questioning during which their ethic would be redefined. Between 1540 and 1563, the Hospitallers successfully prepared themselves to lay claim to new secular glories against a backdrop of rapidly changing political realities in Europe.

In the early sixteenth century, the political climate in Europe was hardly conducive to an itinerant Order of Knights. Most European monarchies, intent on consolidating their kingdoms, agreed on one point: there was to be no tolerance of a state within a state, a danger which was perceived to be integral to the existence of the military orders. Moreover Protestantism, which had erupted in Germany in 1517, made the Knights' ethos appear almost obsolete. The politics of religion developing at the time looked as if they might marginalize any lingering relevance the Hospitallers might have laid claim to.

In 1517, the Augustine monk, Martin Luther, pinned his religious protest against the Church of Rome (known as the Ninety-Nine Theses) onto the door of Wittenburg Cathedral in Germany. This eventually led various parts of Northern Europe to follow a religious path different to that prescribed by the papacy in the South. Max Weber viewed the resulting schism as a prelude to the transfer of the centre of European politics from the Mediterranean to the North, where the foundations of a capitalist ethic would be laid.

However, in the early sixteenth century, the major European powers had not yet fully appreciated the implications of this 'monkish business', as Luther's protest was called by the Medici Pope, Leo X. Mainstream thought remained dominated by the view that each kingdom or territory was to continue to exert authority over its traditional sphere of influence.

In the sixteenth century, the control of the Mediterranean world was keenly contested by three major European powers. In Spain, the alliance forged by the marriage of

Aerial view of Mdina.

Ferdinand, King of Aragon, with Isabella, Queen of Castile, failed to bring complete unification of the country, and Castile and Aragon remained distinct political entities. Castile focused increasingly on the New World, while Aragon embroiled itself in Mediterranean politics, in particular in affirming Spanish influence over Italy. At the same time, the Ottoman Empire was waging battles on two fronts. It was seeking expansion to the East, but at the same time pushing westwards towards penetration of Southern Italy. The third player, apart from Spain and the Ottoman Empire, was France. Under the Valois monarchy, particularly during the reign of Charles VII and his successor Francis I, France fought successive wars to acquire Milan and Naples. Against this complicated backdrop, Charles V, the successor of Maximilian I, as Emperor of the West and heir to the realm of Ferdinand and Isabella of Spain, lent greater value to strengthening his hold on the Mediterranean world than answering to the theological quibbles and political unrest consequent upon the Protestant schism.

Meanwhile, the Hospitallers were becoming virtually a boat people. After the loss of Rhodes, months were passed on board ships, roaming from one European court to another. The newly constructed carrack *St Anne* served as the Grandmaster's headquarters. This floating existence for an Order that for centuries had held its own feet on very solid territories made the acquisition of a new base a pressing necessity. It explains the Hospitallers' itinerary between 1522 and 1530. The Hospitaller's administrative body, or Convent, moved first to Messina, but its sojourn there was short lived. Seeking to remain faithful to their aim of providing hospital care, the Order preferred to move to Cuma near Naples, where the tending of the sick

A street in Mdina.

could be better undertaken. The Knights had in fact evacuated from Rhodes all the sick and the infirm that were in their hospital at the time of the siege. These also included plague-stricken victims. The caves of Cuma, a derelict zone in the port of Naples, became the home of the Knights and their retinue and charges. Subsequently, the Hospitallers' headquarters was transferred to Civitavecchia, thence to Viterbo, Cornetto, Villefranche and finally Nice.

This odyssey brought home to the Hospitallers the changing political climate of Europe, and forced upon them involvement in the religious crisis that pitted Protestants and Catholics against each other. The Order would come to understand that its administrative and constitutional structures had no place within any European kingdom.
This was partly the reason why for the next fifty years, until the 1560s, important members of the Order would envisage that their place was at the heart of the Muslim world, either in the North African town of Tripoli or else in the recapture of Rhodes. Even the donation of Malta, then an inconsequential island in the centre of Mediterranean, seemed not good enough for the Knights. Its geographical position was considered to be too near to a religiously divided Europe and not at the heart of the Ottoman world.

Yet, the defeated Grandmaster, L'Isle Adam, came to understand that the grant of Malta guaranteed survival for his Order. In this backwater, at the extreme end of Christendom, the Hospitallers could maintain their old constitutional structures (which were paradoxically more medieval than modern) and naval practices. L'Isle Adam had perceived correctly that the Hospitallers' survival lay in the defence of endangered outposts of the Christian republic. In this spirit, and as early as 1523, the Grandmaster asked the Holy Roman Emperor Charles V to grant him the Maltese islands and Tripoli. Both sides procrastinated before reaching a settlement. The question of the precise title under which these lands could be held by the Hospitallers, and the barrenness of Malta, were major reasons for the Knights' hesitation.

A first serious exploration of Malta's feasibility occurred in 1524. A commission of *uomini saggi* (knowledgeable men) was sent to the island to report back on its suitability. They were negative about all Malta's man-made structures. To make matters worse, Malta lacked a good water supply and the soil was not evaluated as being very fertile. Its only city was at the centre of the island, and the walls were in a state of dilapidation. Indeed, the whole island lacked proper fortifications. The only positive remark concerned the harbours. Maltese harbours, with their many inlets, were in the eyes of the commissioners a natural haven for ships.

Events in Europe would soon force upon the Hospitallers a quick decision. Initially, the conflict between the Habsburgs and the Valois induced the French knights to oppose taking Malta under the terms of an enfeoffment put forward by the Emperor Charles V in his capacity as King of Spain. This would mean subjection to an enemy of the French monarchy. Then Protestantism complicated matters, as some members of the Order (the Germans in particular) were drawn to the Lutheran cause. The unexpected sack of Rome would bring about a turning point in the Knights' perception of the grant of Malta and Tripoli. When in 1527 Charles V allowed his German pikemen to march into Rome the Knights were at Viterbo. The march on Rome was an offensive aimed at exerting pressure on Pope Clement VII to be more flexible in resolving religious strife between Protestants and Catholics in Europe and to persuade him to accept the convocation of a General Council of the Church, as the Lutherans were demanding. Clement had a personal obligation towards the Order. He was a member of the Order and a former prior of Capua. The bond between the Order and the papacy had been further strengthened before Clement's election, for the death of Clement's predecessor, Leo X occurred when the Knights were in Rome and Cardinals decided to appoint Grandmaster L'Isle Adam as guardian of the Conclave. In recognition, the newly elected Pope, Clement VII, gave the Knights the city of Viterbo. Thus, it fell to them to defend the city from invading German forces. In fact, their stand spared the city from being raided by the Emperor's militia, unlike what happened in Rome, where many innocent civilians were butchered by the Emperor's troops.

The events of 1527 made it clear to many Hospitallers that there was no place for the Order in Europe; Malta and Tripoli represented the only two places where the Order could survive. Malta stood distant from religious conflict on the European mainland, had a good harbour for the fleet and, most importantly, would not resist the imposition of a feudal system of *servitudo marina*, as the island was legally a demesne. Despite its vicinity to Europe, the Knights realised that here they could still continue to perform their mission of the defence of Christian Europe. In the spirit of these ideals, Charles V granted Malta to the Knights as a fiefdom in 1530, which meant that ultimate sovereignty for the islands lay with the Emperor and his viceroy in Sicily. On their part, the Knights exploited the situation by taking full control of all governing bodies on the island.

The Map of Malta published by Jean Quintin d'Autun known as Quintinus in 1533. Wignacourt Museum, Rabat.

The New Home of the Knights

Chapter 4

Religious confrontation in Europe had a profound impact on the Hospitallers. It decreased the revenue of the Common Treasury, as their department of finance was called. The first setback was experienced in Germany, where in 1535 the bailiff and commanders of Brandenburg, following the example of their landgrave, Philip of Hesse, turned Lutheran. With this single move, these German knights deprived the Treasury of the tithes of vast territories in Brandenburg which fell under Philip's jurisdiction. A year later, it was the turn of Henry VIII to seek autonomy from Rome. From a *defensor fidei*, as he had been called by the Pope for his defence of the Catholic Church against Lutheranism, he became the religious orders' most implacable enemy, sanctioning their suppression, the confiscation of their property and even the sacking of their monasteries and their other estates. As a monastic order of the Church, the Order of St John would lose all its properties in England Between 1536 and 1539.

Yet, even as the Order lost territories in the North, it made political gains for having sided with Rome. Most of its commanderies were in those countries, France in particular, which continued to express allegiance to Rome. The acquisition of the island of Malta conditioned further the Hospitaller's choice in favour of Rome. The island, being geographically placed in the south of Europe, made the religious choice more than natural. The imposition and eventual convocation of a General Council of the Church, between 1545 and 1563, would strengthen the Church's hold on those countries that remained faithful to the Catholic dogmas. With this politico-religious background, the mainstream choice within the Hospitaller Order was negatively inclined towards the Convent's placement on the European mainland.

In the context of Conciliar movement, the Hospitaller Order unexpectedly ended up becoming one of the protagonists. The Church lacked the quorum necessary to calling the third and last session of the Council, which was held between 1562 and 1563. The readiness of Grandmaster Jean de la Valette to send his representative saved the Council of Trent's meeting. The necessary quorum was thus possible, but as can be expected, the Order promptly shaped the situation to its advantage. The Order's representative, the Grand Prior of the Church Fra Martin Royas, did his utmost to stand aloof from theological debate. Instead, acting according to the instructions issued from the Convent, he and the other two representatives of the Hospitallers sought to promote a secular image for the Order by using the occasion to obtain the Council's sanction for warring activity against Islam. The paradox was that this plea contradicted the new vision of the spirituality of religious orders as it was being promulgated by the council's decrees, where the concept of a holy war was discredited and religious life became focused primarily on prayer. On the Order's part, the sanctioning of military activity against Islam was accompanied by the rejection of all those brethren who had joined the Protestant cause.

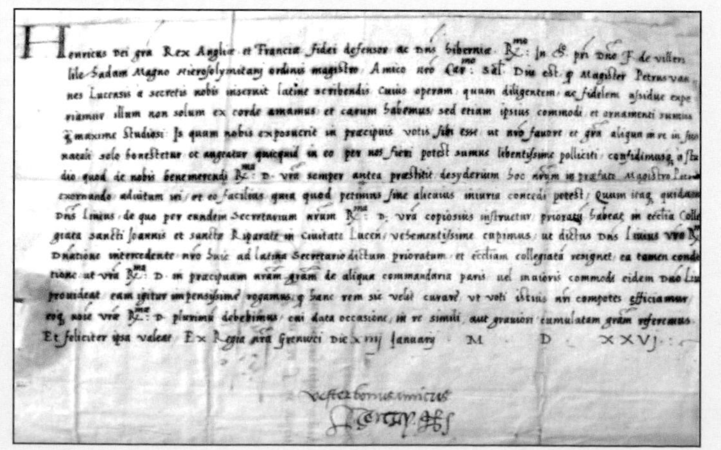

Henricus Dei gra Rex Anglie et Francie fidei defensor ac Dns hibernie Rme: In Xo pri Dno F de villers lile Sadam Magno Hierosolymitani ordinis magistro Amico nro Carmo: Sal. Diu est q Magister Petrus vannes Lucensis a secretis nobis inseruit latine scribendis Cuius operam quum diligentem ac fidelem assidue experiamur illum non solum ex corde amamus et carum habemus sed etiam ipsius commodi et ornamenti summe q maxime studiosi Is quum nobis exposuerit in praecipuis votis sibi esse ut nro favore et gra aliqua in re in suo natali solo honestetur et augeatur quicquid in eo per nos fieri potest sumus libentissime polliciti confidimusq o studio quod de nobis benemerendi Rma: D. vra semper antea praestitit desyderium hoc nrum in praefato Magistro Petro exornando adiutum iri et eo facilius quia quod petimus sine alicuius iniuria concedi potest; Quum itaq quidam Dns Linus de quo per eundem Secretarium nrum Rma: D. vra copiosius instructur prioratum habeat in ecclia Collegiata sancti Joannis et sancte Reparate in Ciuitate Lucen; vehementissime cupimus ut dictus Dns Linus vra Rme Dnatione intercedente nro huic ad latina Secretario dictum prioratum et ecclesiam collegiata resignet ea tamen conditione ut vra Rma: D. in praecipuam nram gram de aliqua commandaria paris uel maioris commodi eidem Dno Lino provideat eam igitur impensissime rogamus q hanc rem sic velit curare vt voti istius nri compotes efficiamur eoq noie vra Rma: D. plurimu debebimus cui data occasione in re simili aut graviori cumulatam gram referemus. Et feliciter ipsa valeat Ex Regia nra Grenwici Die xviij January M D XXVJ

vester bonus amicus

[signature]

A signed letter of King Henry VIII of England to Grandmaster L'Isle Adam. National Library, Valletta.

Despite religious division in Europe, the main preoccupation of Charles V and his son Philip II was the defence of the southern flanks of the

Aerial view of Fort Saint Angelo in Birgu.

Empire, the Mediterranean possessions, and in particular Spain's hold over Italy. Marrying Spanish interest to the defence of Christendom, Charles V switched to the offensive, and the Knights were granted a strategic role in this new policy. In 1531, a year after Malta and Tripoli had been given as a fiefdom to the Hospitallers, the Knights participated in the attack on the Ottoman stronghold of Modone in Greece. A year later, the Hospitallers' galleys were again in action, this time as part of the Christian fleet that captured the Ottoman fort of Coronne. Five years after the donation of Malta and Tripoli to the Knights of St John, Charles V entrusted Admiral Andrea Doria with an attack on Tunis. The Knights were at the vanguard of this expedition. Their three galleys, eighteen brigantines and the carrack *St Anne* were put at the disposal of Admiral Doria. The fleet captured La Goletta and the city of Tunis, thus forcing the Turkish admiral Barbarossa to escape to the Levant.

It is no surprise, therefore, that once in Malta the Hospitallers were active in strengthening their resources, both in naval and military terms. This implied that all the medieval privileges enjoyed by the Maltese had to be curtailed. Ancient laws which would have weakened the authority of the new rulers and their power to implement taxation and legislation were flouted and overruled. The Hospitallers refused to establish the seat of their Convent in the old city of Mdina, which was essentially a castle set amidst a rural environment in the centre of the island. Instead, they preferred to settle in the south-east, in the harbour town of Birgu. Its urban setting, even if somewhat run down in 1530, was more in accordance with their military and naval requirements.

Once possession of Malta was taken, the Hospitallers embarked on strengthening the fortifications, in particular those of Birgu, Mdina and Tripoli. From an early stage, the model of commissioning technical aid from Europe was established. Malta's traditional reliance on Sicily was overturned, and various kinds of assistance and trade were sought in Northern Italy, Provence, Catalonia,

The exterior court of the Castellan's Palace in Fort Saint Angelo.

Germany, Aragon and Castile. An early example of this is the presence in the very first months of the Order's arrival in Malta of a foreign military engineer, who went by the name of Piccino. His mission was to strengthen the harbour's fortifications. Then, in 1535, the Italian engineer Antonio Ferramolino was invited to the island. His mission too was focused predominantly on giving advice as to how best to buttress the fortifications. The same engineer was again in Malta in 1541.

Undoubtedly, the defence issue was a pressing problem. The Knights' arrival had stimulated demographic growth, with the result that the old medieval urban fabric was sorely stretched. With a view to a permanent solution to this problem, Ferramolino proposed the building of a new city on Sciberras Hill (i.e. on the tongue of land opposing Birgu). Yet, the only projects that materialised were the deepening of the ditch separating Saint Angelo from Birgu, and the laying in 1546 of an iron chain, which was tailor made in Venice, whereby entrance to the inlet between Birgu and Senglea was blocked.

On 21 August 1534, Grandmaster L'Isle Adam died and his body was put to rest at the Franciscan Minors' Church at Rabat. Although his successor, the Italian Grandmaster Pietro Del Ponte, reigned only between 1534-1535, the fleet was significantly strengthened since he added a new galley, the *Santa Caterina*. Thus, the Hospitaller fleet rose to four in addition to the ageing carrack, the *Saint Anne*. The latter was a redoubtable floating war machine, with more than 50 cannons, but it needed 500 sailors to man it, as well as 150 soldiers and 100 knights for combat.

The recapture of Coronne by the Muslims in 1534, just a year after its loss to the forces of Charles V, was a proof, if any was needed, of increasing Turkish might at sea. The revival of Turkish naval power would again be felt in 1538 at the battle of Prevesa, fought off the Adriatic coast of Greece. The Hospitallers' galleys participated under the standard of Andrea Doria, but this time the Turkish admiral Barbarossa had the upper hand. The Christian galleys abandoned the field of battle without putting up a fight, thus making it possible for Barbarossa to pound the Neapolitan coast and Sicily at will. Spurred on by these victories, the Turkish and Barbary corsairs operated a number of *razzias* in the 1540s on the Italian and Maltese coasts, which would reach a climax in 1551. In 1547, Torghud

The interior of Saint Anne's chapel in Fort St Angelo, Birgu.

Reis, also known as Dragut, descended on Marsaxlokk, but the Knights engaged the invading force and forced it to retreat. In 1548 and 1550 there were landings in Gozo but they were repulsed. The mounting of military pressure was also being felt in Tripoli. The Order reacted by transporting all the women and children living in its castle of Tripoli to Malta. These were judged to be a liability in case of a siege. Mercenaries were brought over from Messina and assigned to the defence of the castle of Tripoli.

In 1551, a Turkish armada of 100 vessels, carrying a force of 10,000 men under the command of Torghud and Sinan Pasha, arrived in Malta and succeeded in entering

A street in the surviving part of medieval Birgu.

Grandmaster Pierino del Ponte. National Library, Valletta.

the harbour of Marsamxett unhindered. Only small cavalry attacks under the English knight Oliver Upton were organised to deter the invasion. However, for still undetermined reasons, the Barbary corsairs changed their strategy of attack, and instead of marching on Birgu, as one would have expected since it was the most important (yet poorly defended) town, they returned to their boats and sailed northwards in the direction of St Paul's Bay. Here, they disembarked their troops and marched into Mdina. The city was defended by a force of 1,800 soldiers, besides a population of 13,000, mostly villagers who, at the sight of the Torghud's fleet, had rushed to the refuge of the city's fortifications. The siege was short-lived. Again, without any reasonable explanation, except that Torghud might have thought that Mdina was strongly defended by the masses of people visible on the bastions, the corsairs abandoned the siege, directing their attack instead on the island of Gozo. The Maltese defenders felt that they could only attribute their deliverance to a divine intervention, a miracle worked by one of Malta's medieval patron saints, St Agatha.

However, Mdina's relief spelt misfortune for Gozo. The Citadel there was not strongly fortified and had only one gunner. After three days of heavy bombardment, the governor, the German Knight Galatien de Sesse, asked for the terms of surrender. The Ottomans promised to spare the elderly, which de Sesse wrongly interpreted to mean the high dignitaries and nobles, i.e. the elders. Once de Sesse agreed to capitulate, and the doors of the city lay open to the invading corsairs, every one in the Castle (except for those who succeeded in escaping by descending the fortification walls on ropes) was taken into slavery in North Africa and only the elderly, who were more or less valueless on the slave market, were spared captivity.

Encouraged by this success, and with an army that was fresh and eager, Torghud and Sinan Pasha set sail against Tripoli, where another victory was gained with great ease, as the fort fell after a few days of bombardment. The historian H.J.A. Sire attributes the surrender of Tripoli to the betrayal of its governor, the French knight Gaspar de Vallier. According to Sire, Gaspar de Vallier, in compliance with the efforts at mediation of the French ambassador (who happened to be making a stop in Tripoli while on his way to Constantinople) negotiated the truce with Torghud on behalf of the Knights, with the result that all the Knights, who in their majority were Frenchmen, were given a safe passage to Malta. However, the agreed truce excluded all the Maltese and Rhodian soldiers, together with Calabrian mercenaries present at the fort, who were left behind and at the mercy of Torghud (Sire, 66-7).

In previous as in present-day wars, political concessions have long-standing effects. Ten years before, the Ottoman fleet had been offered shelter in the French port of Toulon for the winter of 1543 and 1544 as part of the new alliance reached between the French king and the Ottoman Sultan.
Against the backdrop of this international

political climate, one has to concur with Sire that special arrangements may have been made which favoured the French knights.

This humiliating defeat remained a reprehensible stain for years to come. The poor resistance shamed the Knights, and the treatment meted to the Maltese slaves embarrassed Europe. As a result of travellers' accounts, particularly the writings of the secretary of the French Ambassador to Constantinople Nicola de Nicolay, many Europeans came to learn of the harshness of slave trading in North Africa, and the fate of Christian captives was viewed as intensely humiliating. Nicola de Nicolay wrote: 'I went to see a nearby Turkish market (which they call bazaar) where the wretched Christians taken from the islands of Sicily, Malta and Gozo were being auctioned. Prospective buyers were allowed (according to an old custom of the Western Barbarians) to totally undress the slaves and make them walk naked to

Grandmaster Giovanni D'Homedes. National Library, Valletta.

check for bodily defects. Then, the buyers looked at the teeth and eyes as if the slaves were horses, after which the slaves were sold or bartered or traded by other means' (De Nicholay, 45).

After this fiasco, Pope Julius III suggested to the Order that it should abandon Malta and retreat to Syracuse or Messina. Instead, the Knights preferred to uphold their policy of remaining stationed in the Mediterranean, and recruited the services of the engineer Pietro Prada for military consultations. Prada immediately embarked on the building of two forts, one at the Isola (Senglea) and the other on the tip of Sciberras Peninsula. Prada also strengthened the defensive system of Mdina and Birgu, where ditches and moats were further deepened, while in Gozo the weakened citadel had to be rebuilt. In addition, the Hospitallers planned to reconquer Tripoli. They launched their offensive by attacking the city of Zuara in 1552. Yet the battle was a total failure. The fall of Tripoli had given the Turks the chance to strengthen their position in North Africa. Moreover, they continued to cleverly exploit the feud between the Habsburg and the Valois by strengthening their alliance with the latter. Indeed, after 1552, the Turkish fleet was once again seen supporting the French, this time to suppress a rebellion by the Genoese against the latter's rule by defeating Andrea Doria off the isle of Ponsa.

In this fateful year, the Order hosted the election of a new Grandmaster, as del Ponte's successor, Juan D'Homedes, devastated by the humiliating defeats of 1551, died. The new Grandmaster, Claude de Sengle, took a more thorough approach to the Order's Mediterranean policies. The crushing defeats of 1551 had brought accusations within the Order itself. Grandmaster D'Homedes, a Spaniard, was accused by the Hospitaller's official historian, Giacomo Bosio, of being more concerned with the internal politics of the island particularly in restoring some lost rights to the Maltese and in setting up a new Universitas in Birgu, to the detriment of the island's security. Yet, as noted by H.J.A Sire, the Grandmaster ruled over a divided Order, as his identity as a Spaniard earned him only partial loyalty from the powerful French faction (Sire, 61-65).

Furthermore, the political conflict in Europe conditioned the Order's operations. Even the choice of the new Grandmaster, de Sengle, was largely dictated by strong internal considerations. As a result of the wars between the French and the Spanish, the chosen person had to be an individual capable of guaranteeing political equilibrium between members drawn from these two powers. The candidate had to be an individual able to command full allegiance by all the parties concerned. Claude de Sengle, despite the fact that he was a Frenchman, was considered to be not antagonistic to Spain, and the candidate opposing him, Leone Strozzi, was sidelined in the election to the Grandmastership in view of his political bias in favour of France.

It was under de Sengle's guidance that, on the peninsula of Senglea, Fort Saint Michael was built in 1552 and a bastion erected on the northern flank. However, the part overlooking Birgu was not re-fortified. This was done for two reasons: to maintain easy contact with the latter city in the case of siege, and to prevent, in the case of Senglea falling into enemy hands, its fortifications from being used against Birgu.

De Sengle's period of tenure was overshadowed by one of the biggest natural disasters ever to strike the Maltese islands. On 23 September 1555, Malta was battered by a hurricane.
In an effort to save the fleet from being smashed by the strong winds against the Galley Creek quay, the ships were quickly manned and sailed out of the harbour. During this operation, four galleys capsized and a number of brigantines were lost. Around 600 men drowned, mostly slaves and sailors, but the number also included two knights. Yet, this tragedy gave the Order the opportunity to modernise its fleet. Appeals were launched for European help, which were met by an immediate response.
Philip II of Spain donated two ships to the Order, another vessel was received from Pope Paul IV, while the Grandmaster de Sengle commissioned the building of a new ship. A rising star within the Order, Jean de la Valette, donated a galley, while the Prior of Saint Jailles and the Grand Prior of France donated two vessels respectively.

Opposite, Grandmaster Claude de Sengle. National Library, Valletta.

F. CLAVDIO DELLA SENGLE XLVII. G. MAESTRO DELLA S. RELIG. GEROSOL.
L'espugnazione della Città d'Affrica in Barberia po
se in così alto grado di me rito Fra CLAVDIO DEL
LA SENGLE Generale in quel tempo delle Galee, che
a gran ragione fu poi nell' anno 1553. eletto Gran Maes
tro. Era egli Grande Spedaliere, e Ambasciadore ordinario del
la Religione presso Giulio III. quando giunta in Roma la nuoua della sua esalta
zione, fu con pubbliche allegrezze solennizzata dal Pontefice, il quale uolle riceuerlo in
Concistoro, e poscia splendidamente conuitarlo. Grandi furono ancora gli onori, che rice
uè nel uiaggio in tutti quei Porti, nei quali fu obbligato ritirarsi cacciato dalle borasche del
Mare, e spezialmente in Messina, doue con real magnificenza fu riceuuto. Giunto in Mal
ta tenne un Capitolo Generale, in cui riformò molte leggi, e statuti antichi, che ma
lageuolmente si adattauano all'opportunità di quei tempi, e con dolce, e gentil maniera
introdusse una miglior disciplina nei suoi Religiosi. Ebbe egli un animo nobile, e gene
roso; e ben dimostrollo, allorchè somministrò molta somma di danaro al comun Teso
ro per riparare all'infelice naufragio delle Galee accaduto dentro il Porto di Malta.
Morì alla fine nel 1557. dopo tre anni, undici mesi, e sette giorni di Magistero, auendo
lasciato un douizioso spoglio alla Religione
50

On the death of de Sengle in 1557, the Hospitallers appointed Jean de la Valette as the new Grandmaster. There is not much information about this man's younger days. It is known that he was born in Quercy in Gascony on 4 February 1495. The brief items of information available about his character seem more intended to exalt his bravery, especially due to his sterling services to the Order in the siege of 1565, rather than to present an accurate portrayal. It is known that he had participated in the Turkish siege of Rhodes of 1522, where he was wounded by two arrows. In Malta, his indomitable character was never in question. In the first years, he was twice imprisoned for what the official historian of the Order Giacomo Bosio described as juvenile excesses - *giovanile eccesso*. The reason seems to have been arguments with other Knights, which led him into brawls. Later he fitted out a corsairing galley, but this adventure led him in 1541 to one year in slavery.

This event heightened his will-power. His courage, resolve and suffering were esteemed by many, to the extent that in 1546 he had been appointed Governor of Tripoli. He was to become the penultimate governor, as in 1549 the French knight La Villier took over. After the debacle of 1551, La Valette's climb was rapid, abetted by a wish within the Order for a man of decision. In 1554, he was promoted to the post of Captain General of the fleet. A year later, he was made Grand Commander of the Langue of Provence and in that same year Bailiff of the priory of Saint Jailles. In 1557, he became lieutenant to the Grandmaster. It was a natural step to obtaining the succession on the death of de Sengle.

Yet, the shadows of his turbulent and adventurous younger days would haunt him even after he was elected Grandmaster. In 1558, a year from the Grandmaster's election, the parish priest of Birgu records the birth of a grandson to La Valette. The certificate indicates that during his younger days, probably at the time of the engagements on Rhodes, La Valette was less dutiful in the observance of his vow of chastity than might have been expected.

Opposite, Grandmaster Jean de la Valette. National Library, Valletta.

Immediately after his election and foreseeing that a siege was imminent, La Valette embarked on a new defence programme. In 1558, Malta was visited by another military engineer, Bartolomeo Genga. Genga's sudden death in 1559 induced the Grandmaster to seek the services of another Italian, Baldassare Lanci, who was sent to the island by Duke Cosimo of Florence. Lanci disapproved of Genga's plan for the immediate construction of a new city on the Sciberras peninsula, arguing that there was insufficient time to take the project to completion ahead of the anticipated siege. The Grandmaster's spies in Constantinople were sending pressing signals about an imminent Turkish assault. Instead, Lanci suggested the strengthening of the fortifications of Senglea and Birgu.

Grandmaster La Valette's behaviour during the events leading to the Turkish siege of 1565 support the description given by Victor Mallia Milanes of this individual as 'a man of foresight' with 'a deep sense of rectitude' (Mallia-Milanes, 125). This foresight had developed over years of exposure to Turkish military activity, in particular bitter experiences that took place in the Mediterranean in the 1550s. During that decade, La Valette's naval adventures as the Order's general of the galley squadron pitted him in rather unequal contest with the rapid expansion of the Turkish Empire. In 1553, Torghud laid waste to Pantelleria and Licata. In 1554, a Turkish force landed in Malta and attacked the village of Siggiewi. In 1555, the Spanish foothold at Bougie, a sea-town on the North African coast, fell to Algerian corsairs.

A turning point, however, came with the re-establishment of peace between France and Spain in February 1559 through the Treaty of Cateau-Cambrésis. Spain could thereby give greater attention to the Mediterranean, and the Order was now no longer alone in its struggle against the Crescent. The Grandmaster took this opportunity to propose to the Viceroy of Sicily, the Duke of Medina-Coeli, the reconquest of Tripoli. Unwisely, the Christian forces procrastinated, and only the occupation of the Spanish stronghold of Oran in Morocco by the Ottoman Turks induced the adoption of La Valette's plan. Philip II authorised the expedition but instead of attacking Tripoli, as planned,

FRA GIOVANNI VALLETTA XLVIII. G. MAESTRO DELLA S. RELIG. GEROSOL.
Se mai in alcun tempo ebbe la Religione un Principe prudente
al pari, e ualoroso, questi fu certamente Fra GIOVANNI VAL
LETTA della Lingua di Prouenza, che nel 1557. ascese al Magis
tero. L'edifizio d'una nuoua Città; le fortificazioni fatte all'Isola
del Gozzo; la spedizione di Fra Martino Roias al Concilio di
Trento; la lega stabilita con Filippo II; e le ricche prede di Vascelli ne
mici, furono i suoi primi pensieri, e le sue prime eroiche azioni. Prouuide quindi
abbondantemente di uettouaglie, e munizioni l'Isola di Malta, che poi à 19. di Maggio
del 1565. fu dall'armata di Solimano assalita. Durò questo assedio fino à 12. di Settem
bre, giorno mai sempre memorabile, in cui coll'opportuno soccorso di Filippo II. restò
sconfitta la baldanza Ottomana. L'onore di sì bella uittoria deesi al Gran Maestro,
che più uolte colla picca alla mano difese coraggiosamente i posti più combattuti; per
lo che oltre alle lodi di tutti i Principi Cristiani, ebbe in dono dallo stesso Re Filippo
una ricca spada, e un pugnale, e da Pio IV. gli fu offerta la sagra Porpora, da lui
umilmente ricusata. Finito l'assedio diè principio alla fabbrica della nuoua Città
sul Monte Sceberras, chiamata dal suo nome Valletta, e sotto i gloriosi auspizj di Pio
V. ne pose à 28. di Marzo del 1566. la prima pietra fondamentale. Tenne due Capi=
toli Generali, e dopo undici anni di Magistero morì nel 1568. chiaro ugual=
mente in pace, ed in guerra
51

the small Spanish armada, assisted by the Knights' galleys, occupied Drejba, a small island off the Tunisian coast. The outcome was tragic. Victory was short-lived, as the Turks regrouped and by 1560 had regained Drejba, while the Christian armada assigned to its defence was forced to make a rapid escape to Malta. In that same year, Muslim marauders attacked Gozo again.

The reaction of La Valette to this escalation of violence was to increase Hospitaller activity at sea. Corsairing was becoming increasingly successful, the most important triumph being an engagement in 1561 when a Turkish vessel carrying the Governor of Cairo and a respected female dignitary, thought to have been the wet-nurse of Suleiman the Magnificent, was captured. However such raids only aroused Turkish ire further. Soon, all the energies of the Turkish Sultan would be turned on the island of Malta, as its subjugation became imperative. To besiege Malta was not considered by the Turks as too difficult an endeavour. The Turkish admiralty had extensive information on the island, while the raids of Torghud and other Ottoman corsairs enhanced the valuable information on the island that had already been gathered by Admiral Piri Reis around 1522. Piri Reis had commissioned the detailed charting of all the Mediterranean coast, and this included descriptions of the island of Malta and its harbour, major fortifications and water sources.

Persistent news began to reach European ears in 1564 of an impeding siege on Malta. European diplomats, in particular Venetians, reported on the assembly of a large fleet at Constantinople. Sensitive information began to leak out from Constantinople to Grandmaster La Valette about the extraordinarily busy work at the Ottoman shipyards.

The reports were correct. In December 1564, the war council in Constantinople took its final decision. The next target of the Ottoman offensive was to be Malta. The news was already in La Valette's hands by January. As can be imagined, the Convent was in great panic and in that same month frenetic works were undertaken. Within three months a massive wall, running to about 275 metres, was constructed along the seafront of Senglea, facing to the east the heights of Corradino Hill. The fleet made frequent journeys to Sicily and back, transporting people who could not help in the island's defence but also importing provisions, in particular cargoes of wheat, wine and other provisions bought at stiff prices.

On 9 April 1565, the viceroy, Don Garcia de Toledo, anchored in Malta with 27 galleys. By now Suleiman the Magnificent's intended siege of Malta was an open secret. De Toledo was shown around the island's fortifications. On visiting Fort Saint Elmo, Garcia de Toledo's military engineer advised the Grandmaster to build a ravelin. As the events of the siege would show, this failed to be of any use, as it was the first military post to fall to the Turks within days of the Ottoman disembarkation and turned out to be a burden as it began to be used by the besiegers against the Christian forces.

Don Garcia could only offer assurances to the Grandmaster but little if any real help. He assured the Grandmaster and the Council that in case of attack, they needed only to resist until June, when he would bring his armada to succour Malta. To seal this agreement he left his young son, Fadrique de Toledo, on the island. With hindsight, the most significant outcome of Don Garcia de Toledo's visit was the advice given to the Grandmaster to restrict the council of war to a bare minimum, on the grounds that too many diverse opinions would hamper rather than aid decisiveness. He went on to advise the Grandmaster to take care of his own person as 'the death of the sovereign has too often been the cause of defeat' (Bradford, 48). Don Garcia left Malta without leaving any reinforcements behind him. Besides this practical advice, his biggest contribution lay in helping the Knights relieve the pressure on resources that could be exerted by the elderly and others, in particular women and children, during the siege. They were considered a liability as they could give little contribution to the fighting and strained available provisions. Many old people, women and children were therefore given a free passage to Sicily on Don Garcia's fleet.

The Ottoman Siege of 1565

Chapter 5

The Turkish Armada departed with great pomp from Constantinople on 30 March 1565, but it took more than a month before it reached the shores of Malta. It was sighted on 18 May, when more than 190 vessels were counted, including 158 galleys and three caramousals. The large size of the fleet made the official historian of the Order, Giacomo Bosio, admit that its mass of white sails covered half the horizon. The Turkish standing army consisted of 28,000 fighting men, most of whom were the *asappi*, or soldiers of fortune serving on the galleys, besides 6,300 Janissaries and 6,000 volunteers. The Janissaries were the elite corps of the force. They consisted of the best equipped soldiers and their armaments included long arquebuses. The rest were made up of the *spahis* and the *Iayalars*. The *spahis* or cavalrymen, who according to Fra Vincenzo Anastagi were made up of two groups, were both badly armed. One, hailing mostly from Anatolia, was judged by this knight to be 'the worst riff-raff on earth' (Bonello, 140). A better evaluation was passed on the Greek *spahis*, who were described as "fearless" and yet again described as being so badly armed as to inhibit their effectiveness. They were only given one weapon - a lance or an axe or a scimitar or a similar bladed instrument. Finally, the Turkish forces counted among their ranks the *Iayalars*, or fanatical corps, whose inhalement of drugs, in particular hashish, could work them to a frenzy and make them so oblivious of danger that they were ready to commit acts of folly or extreme bravery for the sake of the cause. Meanwhile archers, by the middle of the sixteenth century, were perceived to be old-fashioned warriors.

Despite controversy over whether the

A general overview of the main engagements of the Siege of Malta; an engraving by Matteo Perez D'Aleccio. National Library, Valletta.

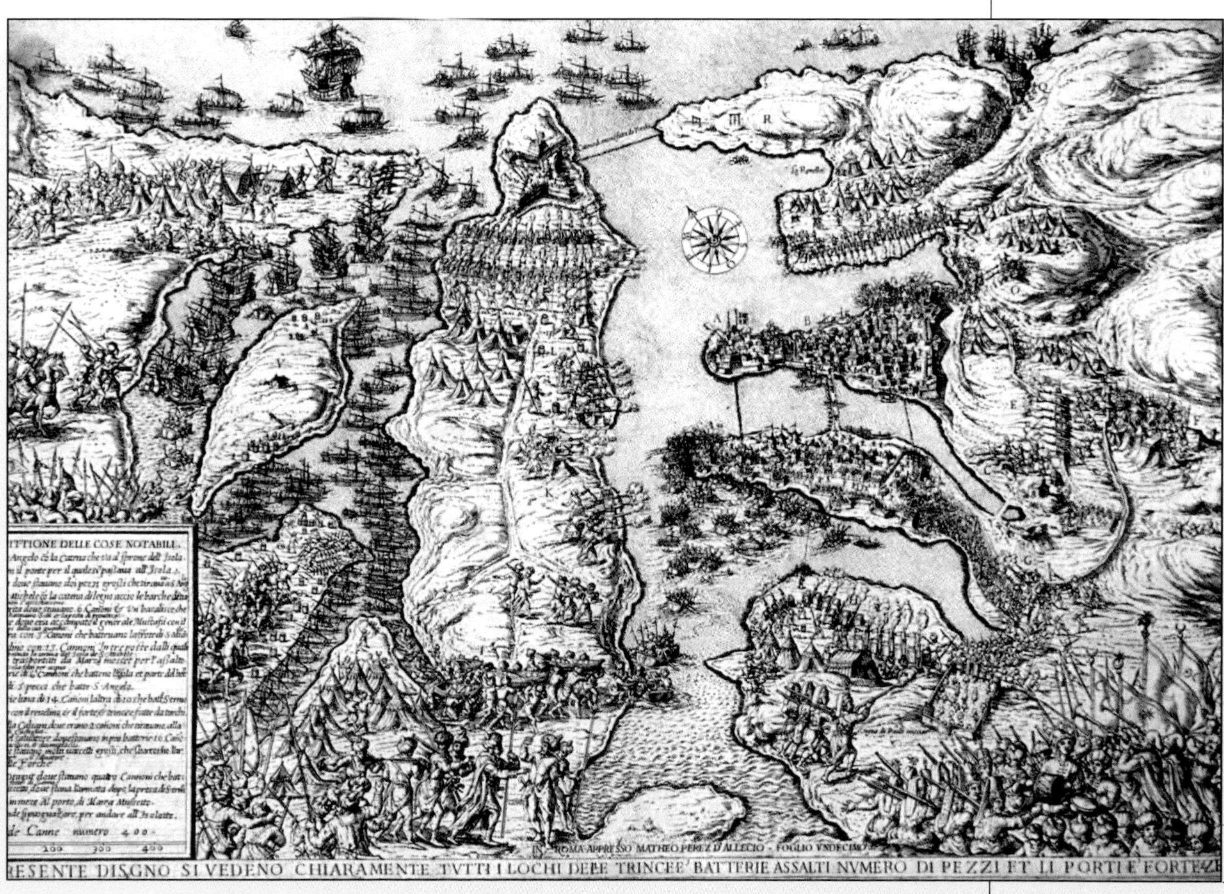

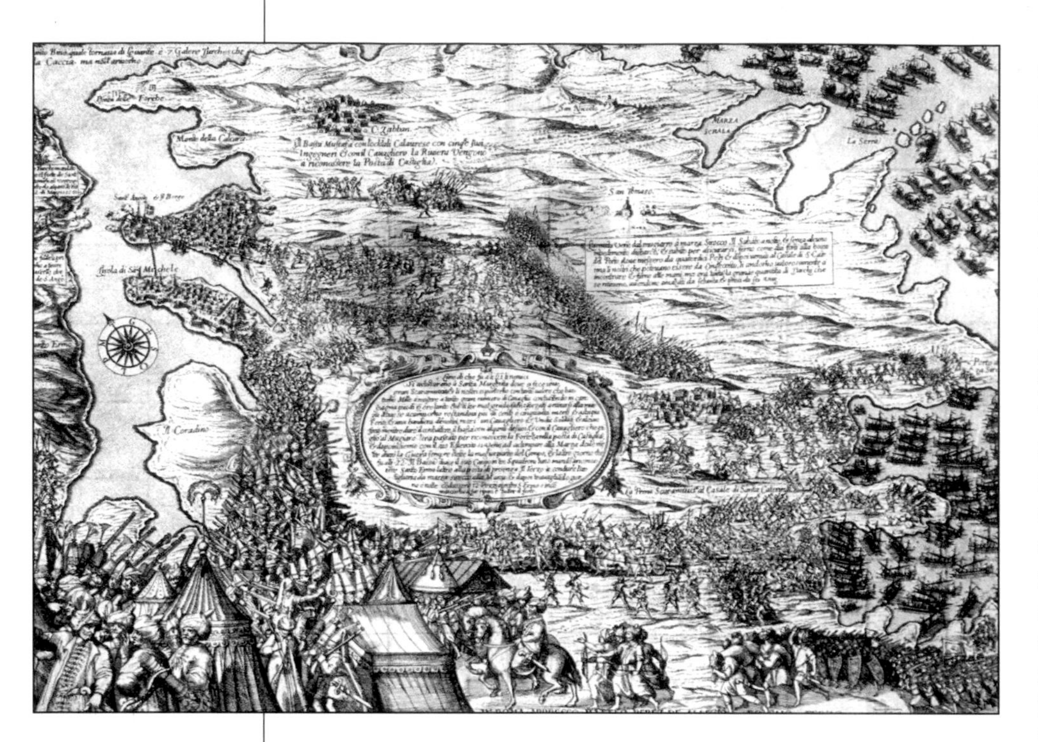

engaged in military conflicts at the time. Two hundred years before, the major battles of the Hundred Years War between England and France were estimated to have involved between 7,000 to 15,000 men. Another factor was that each side could count within its ranks soldiers from different nations and countries, to the extent that both armies formed, to use J.R. Hale's words, 'a motley if not mongrel combination' (Hale, 70).

The arrival of the Turkish Army. Lithograph by Matteo Perez d'Aleccio. National Library, Valletta.

Turkish army was as large as calculated, (some like Anastagi himself, put the Turkish force at around 22,000 men) there can be no doubt that it was a big army from which the Turkish Sultan was expecting a successful expedition. Its size and the anticipation of a long summer campaign meant that the expedition needed supply ships for the carrying of provisions, in particular tents, salted meat and biscuits, besides all the equipment for the construction of platforms and the transportation of heavy military machines.

The local force was much smaller in size. The Hospitaller army in Birgu and the harbour forts was made up of around 3,000 Maltese men-at-arms, 500 knights supported by 500 soldiers enrolled from the galley squadron, 200 Greek soldiers and 400 paid mercenaries, who in their majority were infantrymen from Spain. The cavalry and an additional force of about 2,370 Maltese were stationed at Mdina. A smaller military contingent was posted at the Gozo citadel. In all, a total force of about 9,000 was defending the Maltese islands and had to counter a much bigger force of between 22,000 and 40,000 men. Whatever the size of the besieging army, the forces on both sides reflected the expanding number of soldiers

On receiving the news of the Turkish departure, the Grandmaster had appointed a commission of six knights - two each from the Langues of Spain and Italy and two Frenchmen - to survey the island and report to the Council of War on the likely place of disembarkation of the Armada as well as on any other urgent defence consideration that the Hospitallers needed to attend to.

The defence of Birgu's fortifications was shared by all the Langues. Each Langue was assigned a part of the ramparts to control and defend and on which to raise its own standard. The most exposed was the post of Castile, as it was an advance wall of defence on the landward side of the Birgu peninsula, flanking the city's gate. As the name itself indicates, this rampart was assigned to the Knights coming from this Langue. They were flanked by the three French Langues which held the landward side of Birgu. Aragon defended the westward curtain (overlooking the harbour's entrance) up to Fort Saint Angelo, while the German Langue took up positions in the rest of the line. Such a division guaranteed that the soldiers and knights assigned to each division spoke the same language, an important consideration if proper coordination was to be guaranteed and misunderstanding avoided.

Immediately on its arrival in Malta, on the night of Saturday 19 May, the Ottoman armada sent a galley to reconnoitre Marsaxlokk harbour, a zone that had already been earmarked as a good harbour by the Turkish Admiral Piri Reis around 1525. The publication of other more up to date maps of Malta (from 1533 onwards the Maltese islands became quite a popular subject with European cartographers) certainly enabled the Turks to plan their strategic moves better and identify the key targets, in particular the principal fortifications and distances which all the maps published in the mentioned period represented more or less accurately.

However, rough seas prevented the armada from entering port.
It was forced to continue navigating southwards, but bad weather continued to prevent it from making harbour. As the night was approaching, a decision was taken that the fleet should move northwards and wait for favourable winds to allow it to gain the southern harbours.

It was during this stage, when the ships were trying to approach Malta from a northern direction to head towards the southern ports, that the enemy was sighted from Mdina. A smoke signal alerted the defenders to the danger, and mounted knights and foot soldiers under the command of Fra Vincenzo Anastagi were sent to impede the landing of the troops and equipment. Once the adverse winds forced the Turkish fleet to sail northwards, the cavalry and foot soldiers followed its passage on land.

It harboured for Sunday night in the northern inlets, in particular at Gnejna and Ghajn Tuffieha Bays, but these were too small to receive the whole navy and were too distant from the principal objectives. On the next day, the armada returned to the original place of arrival, Marsaxlokk, where the disembarkation began. The reaction was immediate, as according to an eyewitness, the mercenary Balbi da Corregio, the cavalry sought to disrupt the landing operation as much as possible. But the local force was overcome by the sheer size of the Turkish army.

Fort Saint Elmo.

The choice to anchor at Marsaxlokk meant that the Turkish command sought from the outset of the battle the nearest accessible port to their focal point of attack, the town of Birgu. The Vizier Mustapha Pasha intended a repeat of the strategy used against Rhodes in 1522, and thought to attack the Hospitallers' nerve-centre. Birgu's fall promised the capitulation of supporting military structures and an appreciable lessening in military effort. Harbouring in Marsaxlokk also meant better logistics when it came to the transportation of the machines of war to the site of the battles to come.

On 20 May, disembarkation began in earnest and camp was set up to the south east of Valletta, in present-day Marsa, within earshot of Fort Saint Elmo. Marsa carried a second advantage, which definitely made it a suitable place for encampment, and confirming at the same time that the Turks had quite a good geographical knowledge of the area. It had a running supply of fresh water, which even if not of prime quality, was indispensable for the military endeavour in hand.

The Turks proceeded to establish two other army divisions or *kapikulu* units which were set in liaison with that on Marsa. The latter provided the cohort for the front line of battle. It was supported by an auxiliary force stationed at Corradino, while another army detachment pitched camp on Margarita Hill, overlooking Birgu and Senglea.

Cavalry, under the command of a young Spanish knight, Fra Juan de la Cerda, was sent from Saint Elmo to harass the siege preparations, and skirmishes occurred at Marsa and at Zejtun. However, after six hours of fighting the Maltese force was overwhelmed. At the battle near Zejtun, two knights fell prisoner to the Turks, while the rest were forced to retreat to Marsa. With disregard for the consequences they would personally face, the prisoners misinformed their captors on the weakest points of the fortifications, citing the post of Castile (which had been strongly reinforced on Lanci's advice) as the Achilles heel of Birgu's wall defences. Believing the information to be correct, the Turks immediately launched a massive attack on Birgu, only to be met by strong resistance and a shower of cannon balls and mortars. The Turks suffered heavily in terms of casualties on that day, and vented their frustration and anger on their captives, who were brutally tortured and murdered for furnishing false information.

On the first days of the siege, the local population must have been somewhat perplexed by events. The island's population appears to have been somewhat surprised by the arrival of the Turkish armada, as many Maltese sought the refuge of the fortifications without having had the opportunity to gather the grain harvest or to secure their animals. This, indeed suggests that the Knights, and in particular Grandmaster La Valette, had

The outward fortifications of Senglea, where once Fort Saint Michael stood.

kept the local inhabitants in the dark about the imminent danger. Further, the endogenous population was used to short sieges, and that of 1551 stood out as an example of what to expect from a Muslim armada: a ravishing attack, the resulting *razzia* with people taken into slavery, and after two or three days, a comparative return to normality.

Thus, on hearing the news of the arrival of the enemy, most people living in the south flocked to Birgu, leaving behind most of their belongings and their unattended herds. The thrust on Birgu was so great that the Grandmaster had to order the diversion of some people to Senglea, and some of the most able-bodied men were allocated to Fort Saint Elmo at the tip of the peninsula of present-day Valletta.

The biggest tumult resulted in Mdina. Panic ran high within the fortified city. Once the intention of the besiegers became clear, the population of Mdina seemed doubtful about the military qualities of the commander of the city, Fra Pedro Mesquita; he was judged too old to withstand the fatigue of a siege. Grandmaster la Valette upheld the pleas of the Maltese inhabitants and appointed an assistant to the incumbent, by sending a younger more combative knight, Fra Vincenzo Anastagi, to Mdina. His valour had already been proven when he undertook to pursue the Turkish fleet from land to impede its disembarkation. To strengthen Anastagi's hand, La Valette dispatched a nominal force of six knights and forty soldiers.

However, the available weapons and armaments for the defence of Mdina were scant. According to Anastagi, at Mdina he

One of the outward posts in Birgu defended by the Knights of France.

had 'only two cannons, besides one half-cannon, the half-colubrines… five sacres …and one musket …50 hoes, 60 shovels, 1,000 wicker baskets and ten picks, but no other metalware. There were 120 cannon balls for each gun, 300 for the half-gun, for the half-colubrines 150 each… 60 cantari of coarse gunpowder… 500 arquebuses, though, to tell the truth, only 180 … are worth anything' (Bonello, 146). One cannot imagine how Mdina could have resisted a force of 22,000 men, even if this had been made up of the worse soldiers. The city had enough ammunition for just one day of battle.

It seems that the Grandmaster was somehow informed of the way the Turks were going to proceed in their warring actions. If he held no information he

Opposite, the entrance to Fort Saint Elmo.

showed uncommon acumen, foreseeing that Mdina and Gozo's castle would not be important in the Turkish military plan, and that the effort of the siege would be totally concentrated on the harbour zone. This explains why the bulk of the war material was shared by Birgu, Senglea and Fort Saint Elmo.

The disembarkation of the Turkish troops was in itself a spectacular event which caught the attention of the Christian chronicler, Giacomo Bosio. He could not refrain from admiring its orderliness and organisation. Bosio says that 'after disembarkation, the soldiers formed themselves into a single battalion, which was compactly grouped in the shape of a crescent moon, and started marching towards Santa Margherita. Besides the splendidly rich and colourful costumes, the shining armour, the banners and the standards, they carried a large quantity of other pennants of various colours, so that, seen from afar, the barbaric army looked like a huge, lovely meadow in bloom, pleasing not only the eyes, but also the ears, as various sounds could be heard of exotic musical instruments' (Bosio, 523D, Ganado, 221). On the next day, 21 May, the Turkish commissariat set up its headquarters in Marsa, while a reconnaissance force scouted Birgu's surroundings. They were met by a squad of arquebusiers sent out by La Valette. Meanwhile, the unsuccessful initial attack on the post of Castile in Birgu demonstrated to the Turks the strength of Birgu's fortifications, and may have dictated ensuing policy. It certainly indicated to Mustapha Pasha that the tactics used in Rhodes in 1522, which he had helped to implement, could not be so straightforwardly implemented this time. The following days witnessed extensive digging of trenches on the part of the Turks, the setting up of gabions and the mounting of cannons, including four very heavy pieces of artillery on Saint Margaret Hill in Bormla. Bosio described this battery as 'nearly a fort',(Bosio, 529-30) as it rose as high as the fortifying walls of Birgu. La Valette took immediate measures to counteract this disadvantage. In a period when hand-to-hand fighting was still the norm and when attacks often degenerated into pitched battles, La

Valette ordered the demolition of houses that stood next to the bastions of Birgu to prevent their stones from being used as catapult missiles by the Turks or else turned into a protective shield against Christian fire. Demolition was still going on two days after the disembarkation of the troops.

Probably aware of the great difficulty that his military staff would find in reaching consensus over policy, Suleiman the Magnificent devised a war council for the siege of Malta where collegial decisions could be taken.

At the initial stages of the siege, the general staff of the Turkish army was composed of the general of the land forces, Mustapha Pasha, the *reis* or admiral of the fleet, Ali Piali, and El Louck Aly Fartax, better known in the West as Occhiali, who was a former Dominican friar from Calabira who had switched religion and turned to corsairing. This earned him esteem for he was eventually appointed governor of Alexandria and later on admiral of the Turkish fleet. The Ottoman army had another high profile personage, whose name was El-Louck Aly, and whose nickname was also Occhiali. He was of Greek origin and died fighting during the siege . The make up of the council suggests an imbalance in favour of naval priorities. Indeed, it was made clear to the Vizier Mustapha Pasha that the overriding priority for Suleiman II was safeguarding the fleet, and that the battle on land was on no account to compromise this.

One has to remember that the Ottoman fleet was relatively untried. It was the result of strenuous efforts made by Suleiman at the beginning of his reign to rival Spain. The Sultan had no intention of seeing a thirty-year effort to build a formidable fleet go to waste for the sake of winning a barren island, however strategic, on the periphery of his Empire. The other flanks of the Empire could not be jeopardised for the sake of this one conquest. It was with such considerations in mind that the war council determined the military strategy to follow. It was decided that the first attacks were to focus on the capture of the small Fort Saint Elmo at the entrance of the harbour in order to ensure that the Marsamxett port situated on the other flank of the Sciberras peninsula could be made accessible to the fleet.

Yet an unexpected asset for the Knights was the diarchical government that developed in the Turkish camp, with power uneasily shared between the Vizier Mustapha Pasha and the Reis Piali Pasha. Matters were complicated by the fact that both were related to the Sultan. The former was Suleiman II's brother-in-law and a veteran of the siege of Rhodes. Piali Pasha was also related to the sultan. He was the son-in-law of the Sultan's son and eventual successor, Selim. In the year of the siege, Mustapha was over 65 years old, while Piali was much younger, aged about 45. Despite the fact that Piali was the younger and perhaps the less experienced, he held the upper hand in the war council in consequence of the nature of his relation to the Sultan's favourite son.

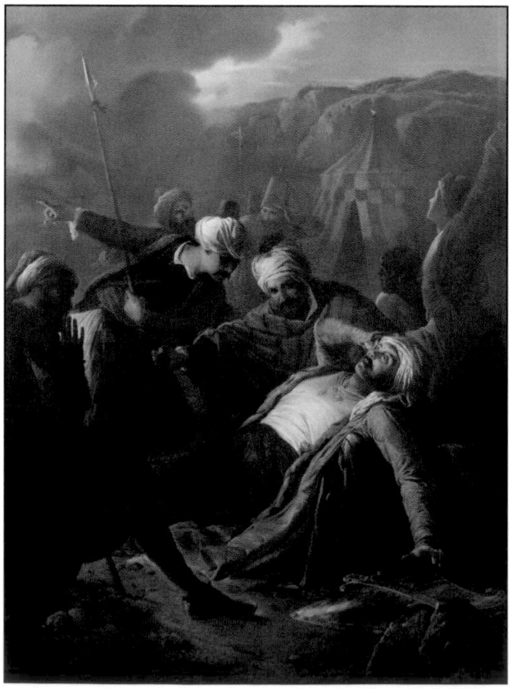

The war council took another important decision that would have great repercussions on the outcome

The death of Torghud. A nineteenth-century romantic representation of the last moments of the North African Rais Torghud after he was mortally wounded by splinters from a cannonball. It is work of the Maltese painter Giuseppe Cali. Museum of Fine Arts, Valletta.

Perez D'Aleccio's painting representing the final assault by the Turks on Fort St Elmo. Presidential Palace, Valletta.

of the siege. They agreed not to wait for Torghud, the corsairing hero of the campaign of 1551 who was supremely well informed about military fortifications on the islands. Instead they embarked on what would result in a long and costly campaign against Fort Saint Elmo. As a result, when Torghud arrived in Malta on 30 May, there was no time to change the already established pattern of the siege. Torghud's serious doubts over the policy of attacking Saint Elmo proved justified, but the initial success of the Turks seemed to vindicate Piali's strategy.

In fact, Piali's plan was not as misguided as some later historians tried to portray it. It respected the Ottoman Turks' priority, which made the conquest of Malta secondary to the safeguarding of the fleet, according to a military logic which was well understood in the sixteenth century. Indeed, a few days before the commencement of hostilities, news of an impeding siege had led to the penning in Naples of an anonymous pamphlet which sought to second guess Turkish military planning and which rightly forecast the course of the siege. The anonymous author thought that the Turks would first seek to attack and win Saint Elmo in order to gain access to Marsamxett harbour. The elimination of Fort Saint Elmo would permit the Turks to attack Fort St Angelo in an encircling movement mounted from land and sea, while the galleys supported the army by shelling the fort from the sea. Having acquired total control over the access to the harbour, the Turks could prevent Hospitaller and other Christian vessels from either entering or exiting the port, effectively enforcing a blockade on Birgu and Senglea.

The implementation of this military strategy was also partly determined by the fact that Fort Saint Elmo and Fort Saint Angelo stood on rather low ground. The decision taken by the Turks to attack first the small Fort of Saint Elmo led them to build on Sciberras Hill a platform, on which cannon batteries were positioned. This allowed them to maximise the advantage offered by the high ground. After some days of heavy bombardment, starting on 27 May, it seemed that Fort Saint Elmo would soon capitulate. On 31 May, the Turks gained the counterscarp of the fort and by 3 June the ravelin, which had been established by Don Garcia's military engineer, was captured. Massive work was undertaken by the Turks to fill

The fall of St Elmo by Matteo Perez d'Aleccio. National Library, Valletta.

ships rushed to its aid. This incident forced Torghud to anchor at what are now known as St Julian's and St George's Bays.

Torghud expressed disagreement with the council's siegecraft. He would have preferred to attack the inner fortifications first: Gozo, then Mdina, culminating in attacks on Senglea and Birgu. Fort Saint Elmo, he thought, would have collapsed naturally after the loss of these forts. However, Torghud was able to adapt himself to the situation. Realising that it would be counterproductive to abandon the conquest of a doomed fort, he decided to intensify the siege by encircling the fort from all sides: first by setting up his battery at Santa Maria point, where modern Sliema lies today, secondly by setting up a battery on the other side of the harbour, at Gallows Point. Torghud's forces were shelling the fort from the Northern and Southern sides, Mustapha's men were firing from the western front while Piali's galleys were bombarding the walls' fort from the eastward side. Yet, despite this new deployment, the Knights continued to successfully send reinforcements under cover of darkness for many days to come.

the ditch of this outward fortification by installing a bridge made out of ten sail masts so that the Turkish soldiers could reach the fort's wall with ease. In the following days, new trenches were dug, and a battery for the cannons was set on the captured ravelin from where the Turks proceeded to shell Fort Saint Elmo from very close quarters. The Turks were now in a position to fire directly onto the fort. Movement inside the fort was restricted, curtailed by the Turkish snipers as they could spot and fire directly at anything that moved within the fortified building. The fort appeared to many to be doomed, its end imminent.

To make the situation worse for the defenders, Turkish might was further increased when in the first week of June, Torghud, now the viceroy of the Turkish sultan in Tripoli, finally arrived with his fleet. His input enhanced the military strategy of the Turks. On his way to making harbour, Torghud sought to demoralise the defenders by parading his ships before Saint Elmo and firing a broadside at the fort. The Order's chronicles record that the fort reacted by opening fire on Torghud's fleet, almost sinking one of the galleys had not other

The setting up of a cannon battery in Sliema and another at Gallows Point meant that Fort Saint Elmo was now open to crossfire from three landward positions; a pounding attack from the front and intensive shelling from points at the mouth of the harbour. The bombardment became more persistent with the passing of days. At the height of the siege, the Turks ranged against the fortifications

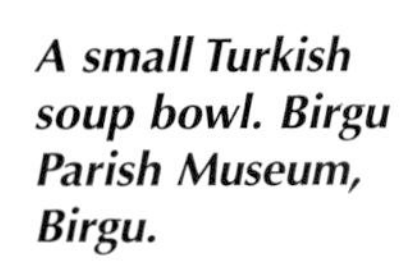

A small Turkish soup bowl. Birgu Parish Museum, Birgu.

A Turkish plate. Birgu Parish Museum, Birgu.

the firepower of thirty-four pieces of artillery, with two lines of ten gun cannons each as well as gigantic cannons known as basilisks. Smaller pieces of artillery were deployed on both tips of the harbour entrance, flanking the fort.

The second major land offensive on Fort Saint Elmo was set for 15 June. Balbi recounts that outside the gates engagements lasted four hours, at the end of which the Turks had to retreat after suffering heavy losses. The attempt was repeated in the afternoon and lasted until dark. On the next day at dawn, under the personal direction of Torghud and Mustapha Pasha, the third ground assault was undertaken. The Turks mounted a coordinated attack on the fort from all sides. The playing of musical instruments, in particular a persistent beating of drums, was used to help demoralise the defenders, and Balbi records that it seemed 'as if the end of the world had come' (Balbi, 78). A seven-hour attack followed, into which the Turks poured successive waves of fresh troops. But all was in vain. The fort and its men halted the incursion. On this day, the Turks lost one thousand men, but more importantly, this reversal forced the military council towards a revision of its plans and tactics. It was during one of the high level meetings held by Mustapha with his *serdar*, as the Turkish military generals were called, that the unexpected happened.

On 18 June, Mustapha together with a group of his *serdar*, which included the corsair Torghud and the Aga (or commander-in-chief) of the Janissaries, were inspecting the Santa Maria battery while discussing military policy when Torghud was mortally wounded by a splinter. One suspects that a gunner from Fort Saint Elmo had directed a salvo at them, after having identified them from their brightly coloured garments. Torghud did not die on the spot. The splinter hit him above the ear, leaving him semi-conscious. He died, according to the Turkish chroniclers, from severe head injuries on the same day that Fort Saint Elmo was conquered. Possibly, the same cannon shot was also responsible for the mortal wounding of the Aga of the Janissaries. Despite these losses, the objective of this high level meeting was fulfilled. Torghud had taken the occasion to invite Mustapha to his camp to explain on the spot how all the lines of communication between Birgu and Saint Elmo had to be broken. He suggested the setting up of new batteries on both Santa Maria Point and Gallows Point just above the water's edge, from where Turkish snipers and gunners could directly fire at any Christian boat that dared to reach or leave the fort. These batteries had the desired effect as they denied the besieged soldiers of Fort Saint Elmo the arrival of reinforcements or supplies from Birgu.

On Friday 22 June, the Turks launched the third fierce attack on Fort Saint Elmo without any fear of having to fight fresh troops fromBirgu. Deprived of the likelihood of reinforcement - the Christian boats had begun to be harassed by

Opposite, the arrival of the first reinforcements to the besieged Hospitaller forces at the beginning of July. Lithograph by Matteo Perez D'Aleccio. National Library, Valletta.

Turkish fire from the newly constructed positions - the besieged prepared to endure a last offensive. The Turks' coordination was now tighter. The eagerness among the Turks that this should be the final assault is evident from the way the attack was conducted. Mustapha Pasha took supreme command and personally directed the offensive. It was an interminable onslaught. It began early in the morning and went on all day, continued throughout the night and into the following day. Pasha ordered the galleys of the dying Torghud and of El Louck Ali, the Bey of Alexandria, as well as another 100 galleys of the Imperial fleet, to assist the efforts of the batteries at the two openings of the harbour and to guard against any boats crossing from Birgu to Saint Elmo with reinforcements. Nonetheless, the defenders succeeded in preventing the besiegers from entering the fort, inflicting heavy casualties to the extent that as sunset of the second day approached, Mustapha was constrained to order a retreat.

It was to be a partial withdrawal. It was not yet sunrise when the Turks were again on the offensive, engaged in what was to be a last triumphant attack on the fort. Chronicles of the dramatic fall of Saint Elmo attest to the fierce fighting and determination on both sides. One should not be surprised that the accounts of the last moments of Fort Saint Elmo are among the most dramatic chronicles of the whole siege. Before the actual fighting began, we are told by Balbi, the surviving knights and soldiers 'resigned themselves to their fate, determined to die in the service of Jesus Christ, and they comforted each other in their hour of agony' (Balbi, 85). In the meanwhile, they received the Holy Sacrament, embraced one another, and encouraged each other with words of consolation as only brave men about to die can use...' (Bradford, 137).

The modality of the attack was again the same as the one of the previous day. Under the command of Vizier Mustapha Pasha, the Turks laid siege to the dilapidated walls and, by noon, had succeeded in capturing by their sheer numbers the spur of the fort. From there they could cross over the bridge.

'Though few and without munitions', Balbi reports, 'this handful of heroes put up a brave defence for four hours.' The Janissaries stormed the fort through the spur and the bridge, throwing 'stones at our men who were defending their end of the bridge', while shouting to the rest of the cohorts to press onto the fort 'because there were none to defend it' (Balbi, 86). By midday, victory appeared to be complete and the attackers, presumably with the shouts of the battle cry "Allah, Allah!", succeeded in crossing over the bridge. The Janissaries rushed to the top part of the castle where they were met by a feeble defence from the last Christian survivors. This Christian force included

Oyster shells in use by the Ottoman Turks as drinking utensils or spoons during the siege. Birgu Parish Musuem, Birgu.

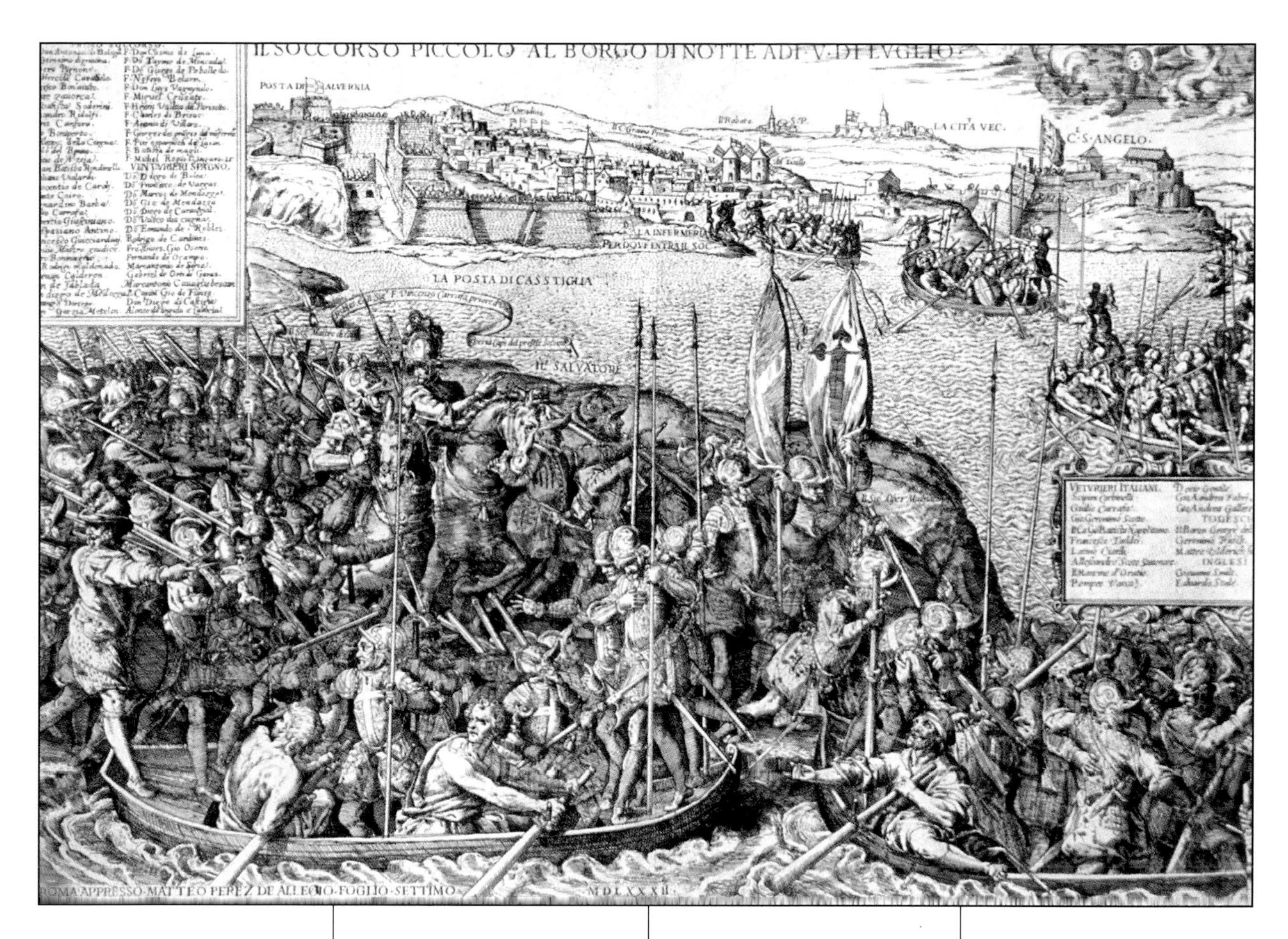

the wounded, who still, according to the Christian chronicler Balbi, found strength and courage to continue fighting. 'Our men', Balbi wrote, 'being very few, and all wounded and hemmed in on all sides, could no longer resist, so they retired to the church (of the castle) in the hope of making a conditional surrender, but, when they saw that the Turks cut off without pity the heads of those who surrendered, they rushed to the square and there sold their lives at a high price' (Balbi, 86). Only nine Knights succeeded in saving their lives in this manner by surrendering to the North African corsairs, who hid them from the Turkish *spahis* and in expectation of a good ransom refused to hand them over to Mustapha. The others either died fighting or were taken prisoner after being overwhelmed by the Spahis, to be eventually butchered on Mustapha's order.

J.R. Hale affirms that all sixteenth-century wars discharged 'an orgasm of terror'(Hale, 27). The siege of 1565 is no exception. Acts of barbarity were committed by both sides. After the fall of Saint Elmo, all the Christian prisoners and even some of the dead bodies found in the fort were beheaded on the order of Mustapha Pasha. Some, with their genitals mutilated, were tied to wooden planks and thrown into the sea in an attempt to instil fear in the defenders of Birgu and impress upon them the kind of end they could expect if surrender was not forthcoming. La Valette, uncowed, responded in kind. He ordered the immediate beheading of all the Turkish and Muslim prisoners of war and had their heads fired onto the Turkish camp.

The one-month siege of Fort Saint Elmo had cost the Turks the loss of 6,000 men and 18,000 cannon balls, and the grievous loss of Torghud. The death toll among the besieged was significantly smaller, 600. The official painter to the Order, Matteo Perez d'Aleccio, in a number of prints propagandistically exalting the Hospitallers' victory, claimed that such losses prompted the general of the Turkish army, Mustapha Pasha, to remark 'What will the parent cost, when the child was won at such price?'(Ganado, 343).

Immediately after the fall of Fort Saint Elmo, at a point when the morale of the Maltese was very low, Mustapha Pasha urged the Maltese of Mdina to surrender, promising that all their privileges would be respected and that they would be granted good trading prospects with the Empire. A similar plea was made to the besieged population of Senglea. They were promised freedom from any ties of servitude that they had been subjected to by the Knights. But, as the Maltese answer was an unequivocal no, Mustapha Pasha moved forward with his plans and turned all his attention to forcing into surrender Fort Saint Angelo and Fort St Michael. Bombardment began immediately after the fall of Saint Elmo on 23 June. Again, batteries were set up on the land flanking and facing the forts. The one at Senglea consisted of at least ten guns. New batteries were also added onto the high ground that surrounds Birgu, at Salvatore Hill, Saint Margaret Hill and Corradino Hill, while troops occupied the hinterland of Birgu, where a hospital was set up. During the assaults on Saint Elmo, the Ottoman hospital had been set up at Marsa, but proved to be too small for the number of casualties. The number of the wounded and sick began to reach such high numbers that many were carried to the ships kept in Marsaxmett and eventually evacuated to Tripoli. To complicate matters for the Turks, dysentery took a high toll. In part, the Turks had expected such a scenario, to the extent that the Marsa hospital ended up being used principally for sicknesses resulting from dysentery. It was an induced epidemic. Once it had clearly appeared that the Turkish Armada was planning for a grand invasion, the Maltese had been assiduous in poisoning wells and cisterns by throwing dead animals into the water. Further, the quality of the water in Marsa indirectly helped the Maltese, as it was never of good quality.

The Turks were also stretched by the logistics of the campaign. Food had to be prepared daily for up to 40,000 men. In their favour was their arrival at the time of the grain harvest season, and the fact that the peasants had had insufficient time to harvest their crops or drive their animals from the farmsteads. Contemporary documentation, in particular siege maps, suggests that the Turkish kitchen relied heavily on the preparation of roasted meat, with numerous carcasses cooked on spits. One particular map also suggests that bakeries had been set up by the Turks, and a big oven was installed between Marsa and Pieta. Yet despite these efforts, the food supply to the Turkish camp seems to have suffered shortages, as Turkish commanders ordered a number of boats to fish the waters around Malta.

However, the Turkish human losses on

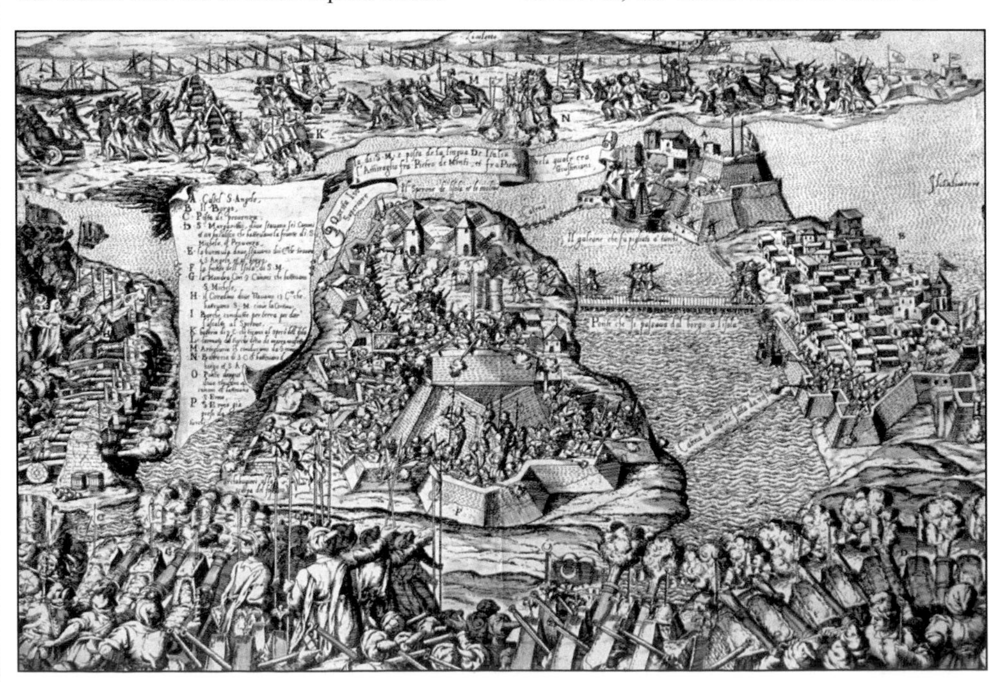

The first general attack on Fort Saint Michael that occurred three days after Fort Saint Elmo had been captured by the Turks. National Library, Valletta.

the capture of Fort Saint Elmo were soon compensated for. On 8 July, the Turks received reinforcements from the Bey of Algiers, Hassan Agà. He arrived in Malta with a force of eight galleys and 21 galliots carrying a force of around 2,500 men, most of them part of the force popularly known as 'the brave Algerians' for their fierce fighting.

Fortune was less sympathetic to the Christian forces. On the next day after the arrival of Bey of Algiers, three Christian galleys reached the shores of Malta from Sicily but the fall of Fort Saint Elmo made it absolutely impossible for them to enter harbour. The garrison of Fort Saint Angelo signalled the impossibility for the Christian force of disembarking, with the consequence that when Garcia de Toledo's galleys were just five miles away from port they had to return to Sicily.

Yet the need for aid remained pressing. Soon Grandmaster La Valette was prompted to despatch a letter to the viceroy Don Garcia de Toledo urgently asking for more aid and insisting that a minimal force of eight galleys should be sent to make the expedition successful. Its successful arrival, La Valette was sure, would bring the siege to an immediate end. However, Don Garcia was not ready to expose a large fleet to the dangers of an open confrontation with the Turks, though the loss of Saint Elmo did induce him to try his luck again and send some aid. Four galleys sailed to assist Malta and this time the squadron succeeded in making harbour, bringing reinforcements of 600 soldiers, 42 knights, 56 gunners and a number of volunteers. On 29 June, they disembarked during the night in the north of the island, and walked to Mdina. The following day, they descended to the Harbour area, until they reached the rocky beach opposite Birgu locally known as Salvatore Hill, where they found boats awaiting them under the command of the valiant knight, Mathurin d'Aux de Lescout, popularly known as Romegas, to transport them to headland of Birgu. The astonishing ease with which the reinforcements seem to have been able to

The assault made by the Turks on Senglea and Birgu, in which they used both land and sea resources, by Matteo Perez D'Aleccio. National Library, Valletta.

where the spur was very low but, from guns placed on the low-level platform, the Christians succeeded in wrecking a number of Turkish boats. More than 800 Turks died on that day alone, while the defenders lost 80 men, among whom was the valiant knight Francesco Zanoguera, commander of the Christian forces in Senglea. His dead body was bitterly fought over by both the Christian soldiers and the Ottoman troops, with the latter anxious to claim it as a war trophy. On this same day the son of Don Garcia de Toledo, Fadrique, who had remained in Malta in token of his father's pledge of aid to Malta, was hit by a Turkish cannon ball and blown to pieces.

It was in this battle that the Maltese engineer Girolamo Cassar earned a name for himself. He showed acumen in the design of military machines when he devised an ingenious method to set on fire the bridge that the Turks were constructing to help them attack Senglea from the sea.

Once the first sea attack was over, the Turks returned to their customary strategy of incessant bombardment before launching their next series of land and seaborne attacks. On 31 July an isolated assault, in which the conquered Fort Saint Elmo was now being employed against the Christians, was launched on Fort St Angelo. The strategy adopted remained the same. A combined land and sea assault was to take place after the opposing party had the defences weakened by continuous bombardment.

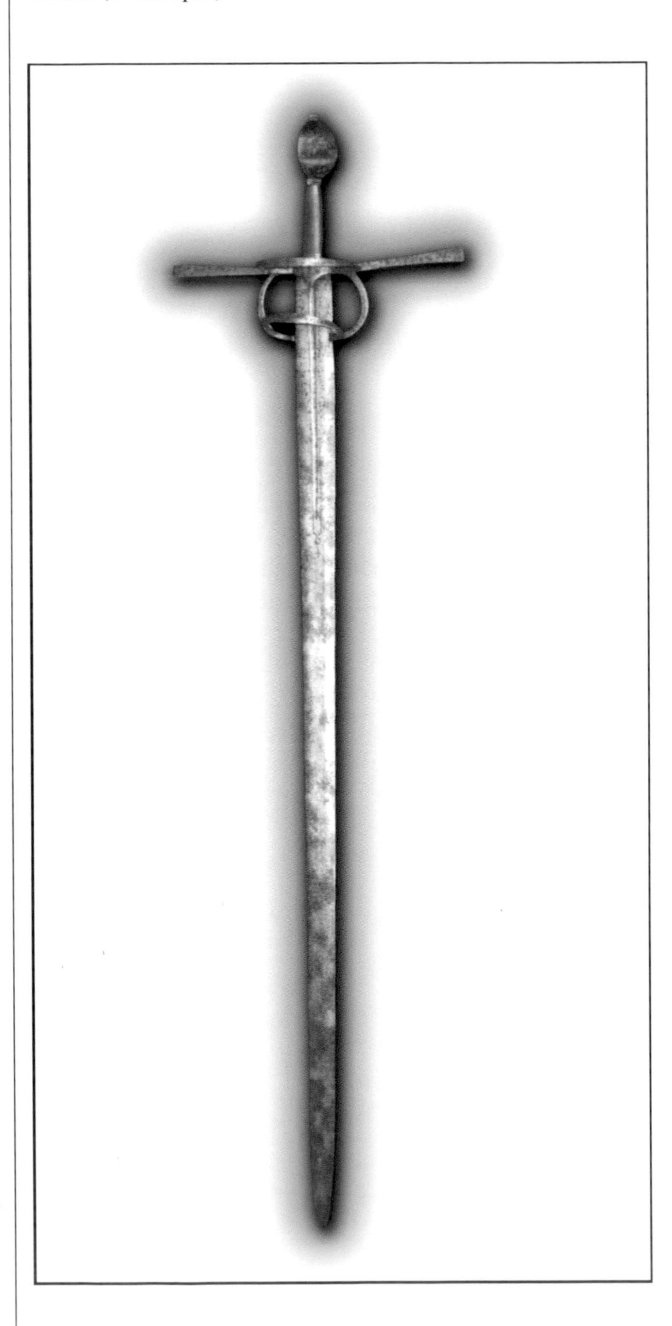

The sword, which is popularly held to have been used by La Valette during the Siege. Birgu Parish Museum.

Mustapha resolved to employ the same tactics used against Saint Elmo, firing on Birgu and Senglea from all sides. However, this operation proved more complicated because of the neck of water separating these two peninsulas.
To address this drawback, Mustapha ordered the setting up of a cannon battery on what is currently known as Bighi, an inlet to the north of Birgu, thus supplementing the withering fire of the cannons stationed on Corradino, Mount Sciberras, Gallows Point and Saint Margaret Hill.
The next major attack on Birgu and Senglea

commenced on 7 August. At daybreak, the post manned by the Knights of Castile in Birgu and Fort St Michael were simultaneously attacked by a force of 4,000 and 8,000 men respectively. Judging from the size of the force, the Turks considered Fort Saint Michael as the more impregnable, or at least as the place that they were hoping to overcome sooner. Birgu was primarily being attacked to keep the Hospitallers jammed on the defensive walls, to deprive them of the possibility of crossing over to Senglea through the wooden bridge that joined these two towns together, and succour their brothers.

In fact, in Senglea, the situation was not encouraging. The Turks had succeeded in breaching the walls and pouring into the city, where a pitched battle developed. Women and children became involved in the skirmish, aiding the regular soldiers by hurling stones and other missiles and preparing boiling oil and even pouring it onto the assailants. The Turkish advance was halted, but it may be speculated that the cause of this reversal had much to do with the attackers' organisation and coordination, which was again found lacking at a critical time. The Turkish assault lasted nine hours and made use of considerable reinforcements; it has been estimated that thousands fell that day. The fighting was so ferocious that fire and smoke could be observed from Mdina. This resulted in a devastating diversion. A cavalry detachment, that for over a week had been waiting for the opportunity to surprise the besiegers, promptly raided the Turkish camp which was poorly guarded, as most of the attackers' forces were engaged in the assault of the forts. The cavalry, which was led by the commander of Mdina, Fra Vincenzo Anastagi, then headed to the Turkish hospital and caused considerable havoc and destruction, killing most of the wounded Turks and a number of able-bodied men.

The attack came at a critical time, when the besiegers were gaining the upper hand, but the counter-attack forced a retreat. The sudden appearance of this force was mistaken by both sides in the conflict as the much awaited *soccorso* from Sicily. The defenders celebrated as if the promised relief had indeed landed, while the Turks rushed to their encampment in Marsa thinking that they needed to mount a resistance to the expected reinforcements from Sicily, only to find that they had been frustrated by a small skirmish organised by the soldiers of Mdina. Mustapha Pasha had to open another front; the dedication of a small force of at least 4,000 men for the annihilation of the Mdina cavalry since, until it remained active, it could mount other surprise raids on the Turkish camp.

Over the next days, Mustapha Pasha, having realised the importance of neutralising these small Christian outposts, handed the responsibility to Piali Pasha to organise an attack on Mdina. Yet the succeeding attack was only half-hearted. It involved a cavalry troop not exceeding 25 horses and an army of 5000 infantrymen. The attack was repelled and the Turkish force retreated to its base at Marsa. The Turkish troops were left with just the option of proceeding to bombard and shell the two forts, and carrying out operations on Birgu before launching another focused

The hat of Grandmaster La Valette. Birgu Pamish Museum.

attack on 18 August.

On 18 August, Mustapha Pasha planned a focused attack on Birgu. Following the continuous bombardment of the previous days, the weakest point of Birgu's defence system was the position held by the Langue of Castile. This outpost was further enfeebled by Egyptian sappers who had successfully tunnelled through the soft Maltese globigerina limestone to a point underneath the post of Castile. Exactly one minute before the general attack was launched, they blew the post up. The tremendous explosion opened a breach in the walls, permitting the Janissaries and *Iayalars* to advance to the first lines of fortification, which they easily passed, reaching the rear lines of Birgu's defences and pouring into the town.

La Valette, who was standing with reserves at the main square in Birgu, rushed to the heart of the battle in aid of the Knights there, and the Fort was preserved. This particular course of action led to his being regarded by contemporary Christian chroniclers as another Hector. The wounds sustained by La Valette during the fighting, for he had one of his legs penetrated by the splinters of a grenade, only served to enhance this heroic aura. The immediate reaction stopped the advance of the Turks and forced them to retreat. Towards evening, they attempted a final onslaught of Birgu and Senglea, but as before, they faced fierce resistance which

The general assault on the Post of Castile. Iconography by Matteo Perez D'Aleccio. National Library, Valletta.

was followed by a general rout on the Turkish side. Nonetheless, on this particular day of fighting, the Grandmaster had good reason to grieve. He had lost his nephew Henri de La Valette in the fight for control of the post of Castile.

On 20 August, the Turks tried their luck again. The Knights were committed to continuing to garrison all their defences. Any talk in some of the Hospitallers' quarters of abandoning Birgu and concentrating all their efforts on the defence of Fort Saint Angelo was met with disapproval by the Grandmaster. Even the idea itself that the Knights could retreat to the fort was not acceptable to La Valette, who immediately ordered that the bridge joining Saint Angelo's castle to the mainland should be blown up. Each and every soldier was pressed into fighting to the last in defence of these two tongues of land. Thus, when another ferocious attack was launched on Fort Saint Michael on 20 August, it was met by heavy musketeer fire. While the soldiers in Senglea were occupied with the defence of the peninsula, Mustapha Pasha moved a high wooden tower; a similar one had been successfully used on the previous attack of Birgu but this time care was taken to reinforce it from below to prevent it from being broken by cannon balls, as had happened with the previous one. On top sat snipers who fired from a higher level on the besiegers behind the walls and embrasures. The unexpected, however, occurred. A group of soldiers led by two Knights crept out of a tunnel dug beneath the crumbling walls of the post of Castile, and assaulted the soldiers guarding the tower. The surprise was such that the tower fell into Christian hands in a few minutes. The capture of this war machine allowed the Order to turn its use on the Turks.

Besides these serious setbacks, the Turks began to feel for the first time the effects of food shortages. Ships were sent to North Africa to fetch provisions, but many were intercepted by Christian corsairs attracted by the promise of bountiful plunder in times of war. In addition, ammunition was running low. Mustapha Pasha had to ensure he had enough ammunition on his ship to see him return home in the eventuality of having to face a naval attack. As a matter of fact, the devastating force of his cannons was slowly being eroded and this was easily noticeable to the Order. The continuous bombardment wore away these weapons and some had even become unserviceable, while others lost some of their effectiveness.

By the end of August, the morale of the Turkish troops was in tatters. Persistent news began to reach the Turkish camp that reinforcements had been mustered in Sicily and Don Garcia's flotilla was preparing to come to the aid of the Order. Pressed for time, the Turks launched another land assault on 21 August, but it was again unsuccessful. In an attempt to discourage deserters (particularly following the escape of some Turkish soldiers to Sicily, but also in order to impede the passage of Don Garcia's ships), the approach to the Grand Harbour was again blocked, this time by a chain of tree trunks and masts. However, gales destroyed this makeshift palisade.

The Turkish command realised that its chances of success depended on securing rapid breakthroughs, and it was at this point that a second and penultimate attempt was made to conquer the city of Mdina, in the hope of strengthening Turkish control of the island ahead of the arrival of Don Garcia's troops. On 31 August, Mdina was attacked, this time by a force of 4,000 men.

The limited number of troops committed to this offensive suggests that Mustapha Pasha was no longer prepared to make profligate use of his resources. He tried his luck again the following day by launching one last attack on the Christian forces holed up in the two peninsulas. But the onslaught was misconceived. It was clear to any onlooker that Mustapha Pasha was now too sparing with his resources for his triumph to be feasible or likely. Once it was remotely clear that victory would not be forthcoming, the attacking army was instructed for the umpteenth time to retreat.

Superiority in numbers was in fact becoming increasingly important for Mustapha Pasha, as he was now concerned with the eventuality of an open engagement upon the landing of fresh troops by Don Garcia de Toledo. Indeed, by September, Mustapha's forces were more and more distracted by the imminent arrival of these reinforcements, and were much less unstinting in their assaults upon the now severely beleaguered bastions.

On 24 August, Don Garcia's relief force gathered in Syracuse, but adverse weather conditions delayed its arrival and the two-day crossing took fourteen long days. It sailed in adverse weather but managed to capture a Turkish ship full of ammunition heading for Malta. On sighting Gozo, the fleet had to turn back towards Sicily to await the gales to die down. It finally reached Malta on 6 September but it was only the next day that Don Garcia's ships succeeded in entering Mellieha Bay, where the troops disembarked at dawn.

Again, Mustapha Pasha miscalculated. On sighting the fleet, he ordered a general retreat. This gave the Knights the chance to regroup and win back critical defensive positions. They were also able to harass

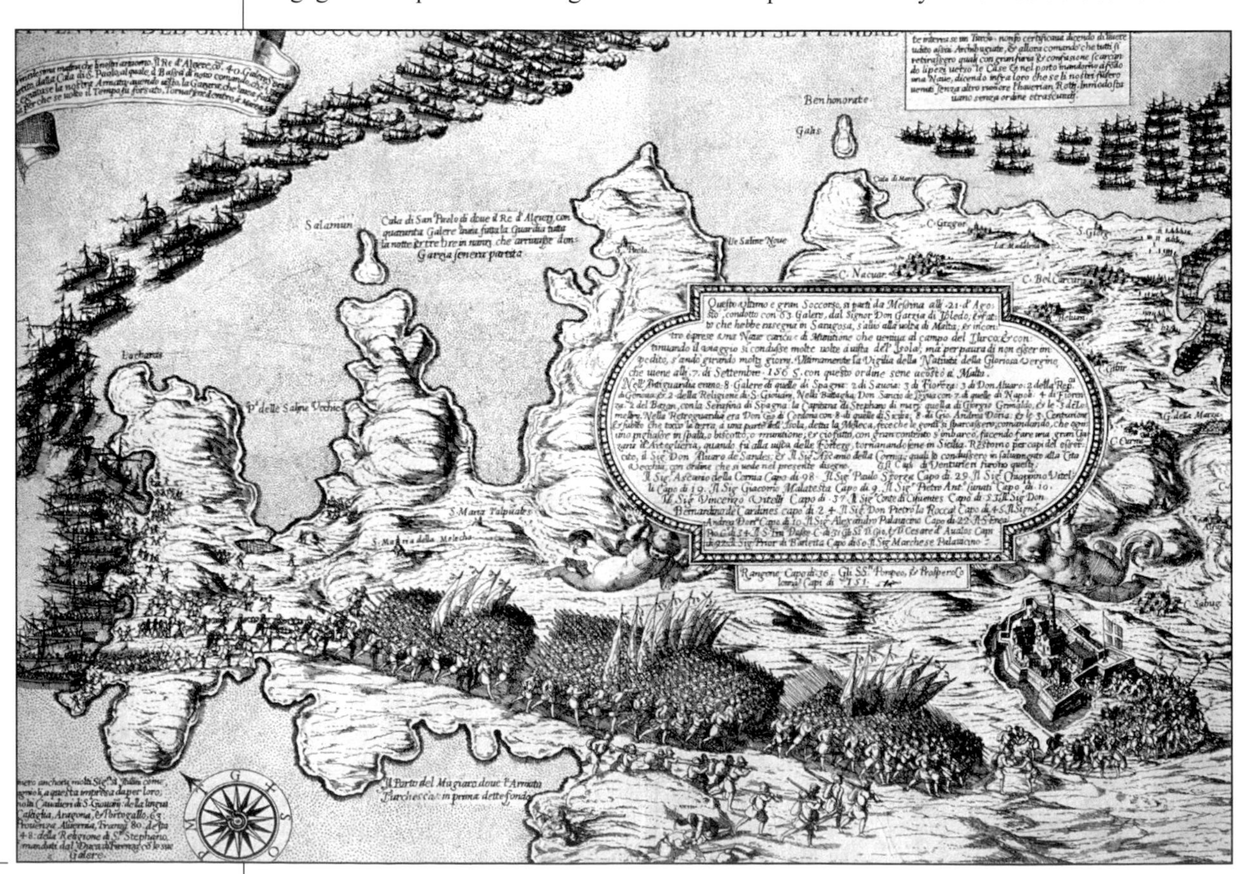

The arrival of the Gran Soccorso of Don Garzia de Toledo from Sicily, by Matteo Perez D'Aleccio. National Library, Valletta.

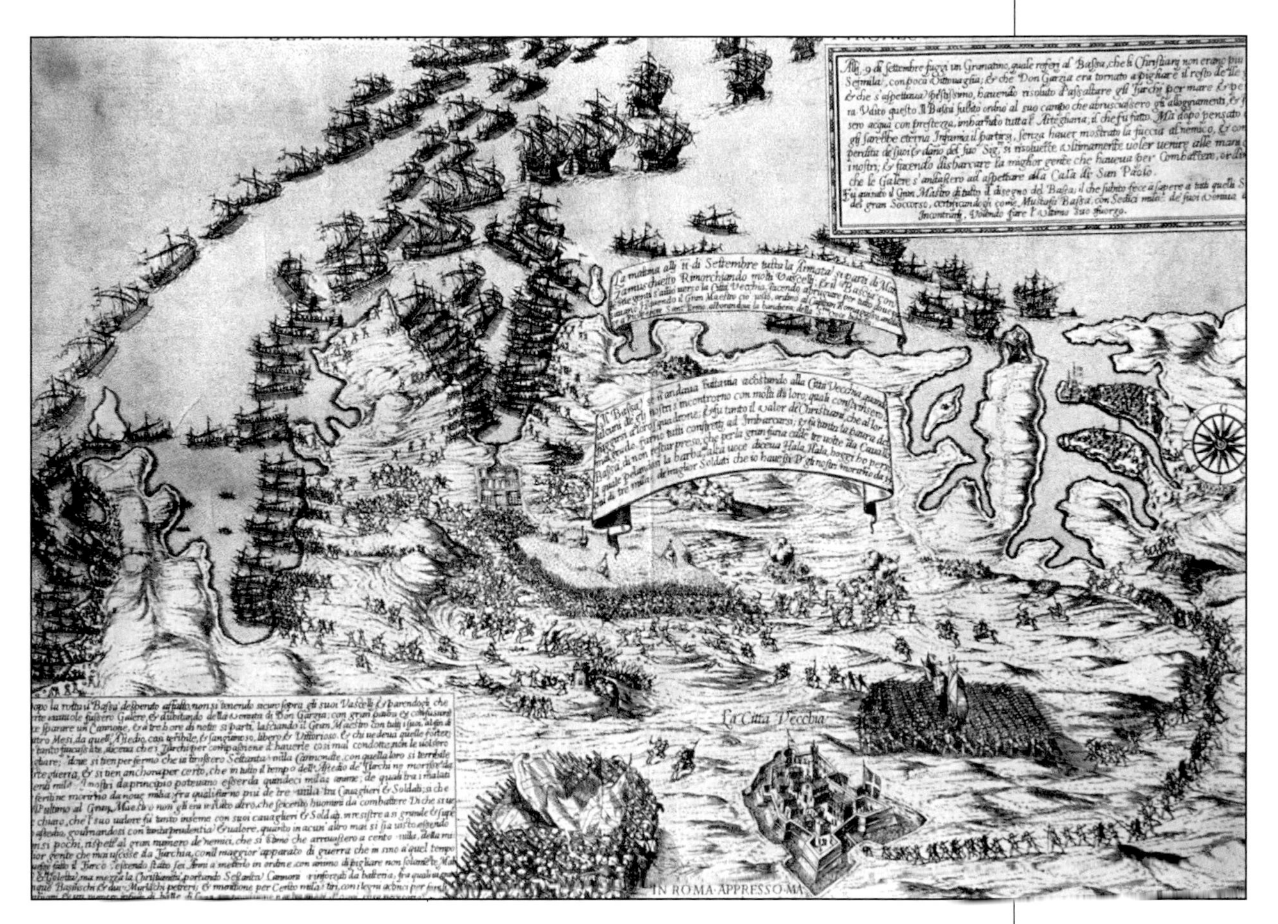

The retreat of the Turkish Armada by Matteo Perez d'Aleccio. National Library, Valletta.

the retreating army. More important still, La Valette seized the opportunity to reoccupy Fort Saint Elmo by sending the knight Romegas to the fort with a new garrison and this decision spelt the defeat of Turkish hopes.

Instead of engaging the disembarked force, the Turks preferred to take to their ships. Undoubtedly, they feared that Don Garcia was intent on their fleet, which was confined at Marsamxett harbour at great risk of being outmanoeuvred and annihilated. Once Mustapha Pasha realised that the reinforcements numbered only around 8,000 soldiers, he changed strategy and ordered his army to disembark and recapture the initiative on land. But it was too late.

The Turkish army's retreat had been precipitous and disorganised. On 8 September, the Turkish camp moved out of Saint Margaret Hill, setting fire to the houses in Bormla that had survived the attacks. On 10 September, the army proceeded to burn all the useless equipment, including old ropes, sails, sacks of wool and materials used in the construction of trenches. The next day, the Turks made one last attempt to retreat with some tangible success to their name. Mustapha Pasha still hoped in a last-ditch victory to repeat the success of 1551, but, instead of attacking Gozo, the attack focused on Mdina. To accomplish at the end of the campaign what had proven so intractable at the start was unrealistic, especially with a force that was by now demoralised by the casualties inflicted upon its ranks.

In the battle for Mdina, the Turks faced the fresh troops brought by Don Garcia, most of whom were Spanish mercenaries. To shouts of the word "Santiago", (a reference to the Spanish shrine of Santiago of Compostella) they opened fire and even descended on the enemy, provoking havoc and great destruction to the extent that the opposing ranks were completely broken. The retreat was a complete disaster. Balbi

Sixteenth-century harquebuses. The Armoury, Valletta.

records that 'those who could not get into the boats threw themselves into the sea and, wounded and tired, were drowned before they could reach the galley' (Balbi, 117). Despite this success, Don Garcia continued to act with extreme caution, to the extent that this trait of his was now becoming proverbial. He forbade his army from pressing home the advantage and was unwilling that his fleet should get engaged in battle on the open seas. Hundreds of Turks nevertheless lost their lives after being pursued by Maltese forces stationed on the higher ground overlooking St Paul's Bay, where the disembarkation and re-embarkation operation took place. Indeed, corpses were still afloat in the bay weeks after the end of the siege. However, Don Garcia de Toledo's caution gave the Turks two days' respite, facilitating their embarkation and eventual retreat on 13 September.

Cannonballs used during the siege of 1565. Birgu Parish Museum, Birgu.

In a map published in Lyon on 10 November 1565 to commemorate the Christians' victory, the cartographer Pierre Woieriot de Bouzey, who claims to have been present during the siege, gave a succinct resume of the Turkish army's defeat, which summarises the general losses suffered by the Turks in these three months of battle.

'The Ottoman army had been reduced to twenty-eight thousand, with many either killed in battle or dead from their wounds. It is certain that out of five thousand Janissaries, only one thousand five hundred were left, and only three thousand out of twelve thousand *spahis*. Out of ten thousand adventurers only five

thousand survived… As regards the force from Tripoli, it lost its leader, Torghud, together with the greater part of his men. Of the force from Algiers, many also went missing and they left in a weak condition. On the Christian side, three hundred and thirteen knights of Malta lost their lives in the siege and eighty were wounded. Of the rest of the population, it is certain that nine thousand died, mostly through gunfire… The Turks had left behind them in Malta twenty-four bronze siege guns…They had bombarded Saint Elmo, Saint Michael and Borgo with seventy-eight guns and six remarkable basilisks. In total, they fired against us eighty-eight thousand shots. No more spars of galleys or other vessels are left, and all the sails, tents and mattresses have disappeared as we had to use them as fascines for the repair of the fortifications; and, whatever repairs we carried out during the night, were destroyed by the Turks the morning after' (Ganado, 207).

In Malta, commemoration of the siege has survived up to this day. The Grandmaster's order that victory was to be remembered each year with great religious solemnity, with the day set aside for special commemoration established as 8 September, is one that is still upheld. This is also the day in the Roman Catholic liturgy when the feast of the Nativity of Mary is celebrated, and indeed despite the fact that the Turkish armada departed definitively from Malta on 13 September, it was widely believed at the time that the true cause of victory over the Turks arose from the intercession of the Virgin Mary on the day commemorating Her birth.

Turkish lead gunpowder measurements. Birgu Parish Museum, Birgu.

A Turkish oil lamp used during the Siege of Malta. Birgu Parish Museum, Birgu.

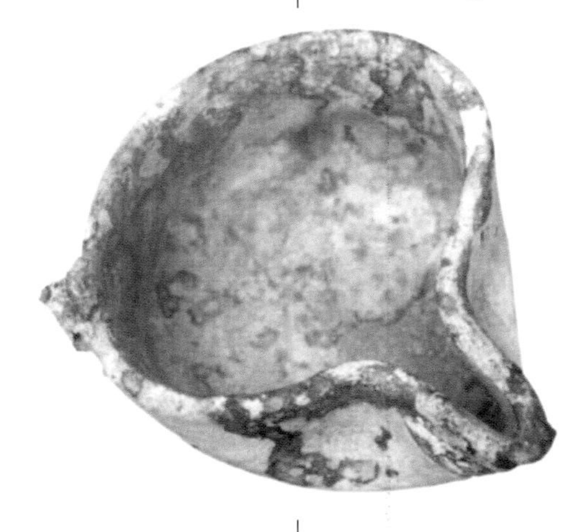

The Inheritance of War

Chapter 6

Contrary to the tendency of the local historiographic tradition to construct the Great Siege as a significant setback for the Ottoman Empire, the events of 1565 could with some justification be viewed as a not unsuccessful campaign for the Turks. This can be understood in the context of the Ottoman Empire's drive to move its massive fleet from the Eastern to the Central Mediterranean more or less unhindered and within a relatively short period of time. Indeed, it was not generally part of Ottoman policy for maritime manoeuvres to be crowned by land conquest, though looting and enslavement were certainly frequent objectives. And while there can be no doubt that the siege was a very deliberate military undertaking, it is debatable whether the Turks envisaged or hoped for any long-term consequences to emerge from their campaign. Suleiman was of the opinion that this siege had to be the stepping-stone for the conquest of Sicily, but as I shall be showing in this chapter there were other important motives which could have pushed the Sultan towards this venture. The overriding important consideration was for the navy to avoid severe material damage. Any territorial gains were in this sense an added value to the mission dispatched from Suleiman's throne.

Whatever the perspective through which the siege is viewed, however, the major losses incurred by the Turks, both in terms of losses within the ranks and economic reversals, are hard to overlook. It was reported by European ambassadors in Constantinople that each and every family living in the city suffered the loss of a close relative or friend. The economic consequences are less evident, as they were absorbed within the Turkish military machine's efforts to remain well geared for war despite the setback in Malta. It may be indicative, however, that in 1566 Egypt, which was then under Ottoman control, registered strong inflationary pressures which had negative consequences not only in Egypt but in the whole region. Interestingly, the French historian Fernand Braudel suggests the possibility of a link between the siege of Malta of 1565 and the worsening economic situation in Egypt, suggesting also that the prolonged strain of the siege of Malta 'marked the first sign of exhaustion of the Turkish Empire' (Braudel, 539).

It must be said, however, that in 1566 and immediately afterwards the Maltese economy was not faring much better than Egypt's. Malta lacked the resources necessary for rapid regeneration. The siege had devastated the island both physically and economically. The urban centres around the harbour faced ruin. Historians often mention Birgu as the urban region to have suffered most during the siege, but one cannot forget the damage wreaked upon the towns of Senglea and Bormla, which had already established themselves before the siege, or upon the area spread below Fort Saint Elmo. And, in economic terms, the preparations for the siege and the defence itself severely weakened the island, emptying the Order's coffers.

Maltese historiography's references to the military preparations undertaken in the years prior to the siege occasionally give the impression that they were the outcome of long-term planning. However, the projects proposed by leading Italian military engineers were more often than not shelved for lack of resources or, where undertaken, were partly or poorly executed. Furthermore, until the first half of the sixteenth century it was not yet customary for the European powers to prepare well ahead against any eventual Ottoman invasion. The French monarchy, for instance, preferred to replace a policy of belligerence and continued hostility with one of maintaining a privileged relationship with the Turks. Venice opted for some form of economic partnership with the Sublime Porte through which it guaranteed the access to Levantine trade and the spice route. Meanwhile Spain, the Papacy and a number of Italian Duchies were more readily aggressive, but they nevertheless avoided allocating substantial funds to defence. Instead they considered it more expedient to invest in espionage, in order to anticipate the targets and thrusts of the Turks and be ready to mount quick counters by mobilising mercenary armies and reinforcing fortification systems.

This latter option was put to work in Malta; as was explained in the previous chapters, mercenaries were quickly conveyed to the island while the peninsula of Senglea had a cordon of walls constructed around it within a few months. Additionally, the Christian powers placed great faith in their military technology, and indeed Malta was to import massive amounts of gunpowder and other weaponry from Florence, which was known during this period as a reliable and leading furnisher of such goods. These three factors no doubt contributed to the Order's success in repelling the invasion, but they also left it and indeed the island as a whole in dire financial straits.

For these reasons, it is appropriate to modulate any discourse that celebrates the Order's achievements in the siege with the recognition that, on their withdrawal, the Ottoman force left behind it a devastated island and a bankrupted administration. In this sense, the Knights were also the losers. In economic and military terms, at least, the Turks were still strong, whereas the situation was different in Malta. The Island could not have survived had assistance from Europe not been forthcoming. It was only as a result of such assistance (on which I shall dwell further in the next chapter) that the Knights succeeded in securing a brighter future both for their tenancy of the island and for the population.

Some words on the motivation behind the siege are also pertinent. In Chapter 4, I delved into the explanations of the reasons for the siege given by those commentating at the time. The main explanation, advanced among others by one of the mercenary soldiers, Balbi Di Corregio, was that the siege was an outcome of and retaliation against the Knights' corsairing incursions in the Levant. On their part, the Knights had a vested interest in ensuring that the siege came to be viewed as a preliminary to the Ottoman attempt to conquer Western Europe. This view was encouraged by Grandmaster La Valette himself, in an attempt to secure greater assistance from European monarchs. However, there is another factor which has not yet been adequately explored; this concerns the economic circumstances of the Ottoman Empire. The siege occurred towards the end of Suleiman's reign, at a time when Constantinople had grown into one of the leading cities in the Mediterranean, as well as the most densely populated. Suleiman brought significant wealth to his Empire and the city of Constantinople in particular, but such enviable prosperity was not easy to sustain, and recessionary pressures could not be ignored. It is a fact that wars were regarded by Imperial rulers as a stimulator for an upward economic trend. In the past, theoreticians constantly argued that wars brought the re-strengthening of the countries' decaying morals, besides an economic and a cultural revival. Moreover, periods of economic decline were usually the cause for the have-nots to become poorer but the rich to grow richer. A massive siege could have rid Constantinople of some of the strain on the demand for food and other resources. Was the siege of Malta intended to recreate a new economic, social and moral order in Constantinople? The answer must lie in the surviving historical archives of Istanbul and the other Turkish cities.

Most of the siege accounts terminate with the story of the retreat of the Turkish army, detailing losses among the standing forces but without entering into any discussion of the short- and long term effects of the conflict on the local population. The reason for this omission may be linked to the perceptions of sixteenth-century rulers about the cheapness of soldiers' lives, regarded as little better than that of 'caterpillars and grasshoppers that eat the buds of the earth' (Hale, 84). This, said by Charles V of his soldiers, in part explains why most of the siege victims on the Christian side remained unbemedalled and uncompensated, with their usual fate being a shovelling into mass graves. Even worse was the fate reserved for the enemy's corpses. Many were left lying on the ground to be devoured by roaming animals. Better post-engagement conditions prevailed within the Turkish ranks. Contrary to the Christian camp, the Turks kept a campaign register where the death of the most valiant, irrespective of their rank, was recorded. The military efforts, strains and fatigue endured by the minor soldiers were more appreciated. Throughout the siege of Malta, valiant Turkish soldiers received *timars*, or land

implication would be that around one fourth of the population perished.

The catastrophic effects of war on women are again apparent in these Church registers. The marriage pattern changed in the years immediately following the siege. The female age at first marriage fell drastically and a number of females were found marrying below the age of twelve, some even at the age of eight. Similar studies undertaken on particular periods have shown that about 25 per cent of the brides were getting married below the age of 15. Such a percentage was normally reached in Malta during extreme crises, as in the case of the plague epidemic in 1675. In normal situations, throughout the first half of the seventeenth century the percentage of brides below the age of 15 reached 12 per cent of the total. Such specific calculations are impossible to make for the middle of the sixteenth century, as the records lack the age-at-marriage of the spouses. Despite the scant information, it is possible to forecast that the percentage of young brides would again have been relatively high. In fact, some reconstruction of the age-at-marriage becomes already possible for the first decade after the siege, by undertaking a comparative review of the marriage acts of the spouses and their baptismal records. This makes it possible to derive the age at marriage. Instances of girls marrying even below the age of ten have been encountered both in post-siege Birgu as well as in the surrounding villages. These early marriages imply strong social pressures that could in part have resulted from the demographic crisis of the time.

In such a scenario, one also expects a gender imbalance. For men, the risk of mortality in sixteenth-century conflicts was high, as they were expected to be on the front-line of battle. An imbalance in the relative gender ratio was thus probable, and this might be expected to have affected mostly women within the marriageable age of 15 and 45. It should here be remembered that though the age at marriage, in particular among women, tended to be younger than normal, widows might have been expected to find it more difficult to remarry. Yet, the situation seems to have been different in Malta. The matrimonial acts of remarrying spouses seem to suggest out that widows were the preferred partners for child-rearing fathers who had lost their wives during times of crisis.

Until now, the discussion has focused on the Knights' military activities, sidelining the fact that their management of peacetime proved historically fundamental for the Maltese Islands' development. Indeed, war was not always the worst collective crisis. Once the euphoria of victory was over, the siege was overtaken by more terrifying mishaps. In fact, Hospitaller Malta would suffer from periods of extreme famine, in particular between 1587 and 1591, and between 1599 and 1603; it was also visited twice by severe outbreaks of plague in 1592-3 and 1675-6.

MDLXV

The Great Siege Monument in Valletta. The work of the Maltese sculptor Antonio Sciortino.

Internal Strife after the Siege

Chapter 7

News of the Hospitallers' victory spread throughout Europe, with the Hospitallers making judicious use of the printing medium to publicise their triumph. Despite the fact that such an achievement risked being construed as a Popish victory, it brought rejoicing from both Catholic and Protestant monarchs. This was expressed also through the bestowal of handsome gifts upon Grandmaster La Valette, who astutely encouraged the view that the victory was entirely the Order's, thereby downplaying the role of Don Garcia de Toledo. The Grandmaster and the Hospitallers' historians portrayed the latter in a very bad light, accusing him of procrastination and hesitancy in coming to the assistance of the Order.

Map of Valletta's cityscape. National Library, Valletta.

The victory of 1565 persuaded the Order to give up thoughts of a resettlement in Rhodes or Tripoli. Malta was now their home. Another important decision followed upon this. Once the euphoria of victory was overtaken by sober assessment of what needed to be done, the Grandmaster announced plans for the building of a new city on the barren ground of Sciberras Peninsula. The European monarchies were asked to tangibly express their recognition of the Order's success by materially contributing to the building of this new city. The appeal did not fall on deaf ears. Cash and equipment made its way to Malta from most of the Christian monarchies. The Emperor Maximilian II donated 300 gold scudi. Pope Pius V sent one of his architects, Francesco Laparelli, to help with the designs and also donated 5000 gold scudi. Philip II of Spain put up 20,000 scudi worth of aid, the king of Portugal, Dom Sebastian, donated 30,000 Portughese cruzad, while various Italian duchies sent ammunition to Malta.

The time taken for the funds to reach Malta, coupled with the distractions occasioned by fear that the Turks might be about to embark on another siege, delayed the implementation of the project. Nor were the Order's fears unjustified. The Turks were in fact re-arming for a new campaign, but the chosen target was not Malta. Instead they preferred to attack Central Europe, and in 1566 Suleiman II personally moved his army on the fortress of Szigeth in Hungary.

In 1566, the building of the new city was assigned to the architect Francesco Laparelli from Cortona, who after long discussions proposed a grid pattern for the new city. In the event, La Valette did not live to see the new city completed, as he died in 1568. It fell to his successor, the Italian Pietro del Monte, to oversee the first stages of the work's completion. Del Monte acted with great decisiveness. He immediately ordered the Hospitaller Convent to be transferred from Birgu to Valletta. Any potential resistance to relocation was thereby nipped in the bud, as the faction opposed to the move was faced with a *fait accompli*. Moreover, the Order had every interest to see the construction of their auberges and palaces completed if they were to continue living in the style they were accustomed to. Those who procrastinated, it has been claimed, were ordered to shift residence to Valletta and forced to live under tents until their new home was ready.

Del Monte also made a priority of defence issues. Formidable fortifications were raised on the peninsula on which the city would be constructed. They observed contemporary ideas on military architecture, with flanks installed on both sides of the main gate. Two massive cavaliers, or towers, were planned, while Fort Saint Elmo was rebuilt in the form of a star.

Portrait of Pietro Del Monte. Wignacourt Museum, Rabat.

During the reign of the following Grandmaster, the French Jean Levesque de la Cassière, other less militaristic constructions got under way. La Cassière commissioned the Maltese architect Girolamo Cassar to design most of Valletta's early palaces, and entrusted him with overseeing the execution of the plan of the new Conventual Church dedicated to Saint John. It was in La Cassière's time that the new hospital, or Sacra Infermeria, as it was known by the Knights, was built at the tip of the peninsula, overlooking the entrance to the harbour.

Yet, La Cassière's rule would be mostly remembered for serious internal conflict within the Order. So intense was the friction that some of the parties involved appealed to Rome, asking that their case be judged by the Pope himself. The clashes mirrored larger conflicts in Europe. The Knights' early years in Malta had been characterised by brawls in Birgu between Spanish and French brethren, making this small harbour a microcosm of division between the Spanish and French monarchies. These internal hostilities were temporarily suspended in the face of a common enemy in 1565 but resurfaced thereafter. La Valette had to endure a rebellion within the Order in 1568, when Castilian knights reacted intemperately to a number of restrictions imposed by him. They stormed into the Council Hall of the Magisterial Palace, ransacked the building, threw the Chancellor's desk out of the window, and then sought refuge in Sicily to escape punishment. Tension mounted in the coming years, and the election of the Italian del Monte calmed matters only temporarily. Things came to a head during La Cassière's term of office. The conflict degenerated into a personal confrontation between the Grandmaster and another French knight, Romegas, who like La Cassière was a siege hero, leading to the removal of the Grandmaster from office. Behind this clash of personalities, linked in part with the unfulfilled wish of Romegas to be elected Grandmaster, lay

A street in the Collacchio area of Birgu.

the shadow of European politics.
By the 1570s, French politics were dominated by the rift between the Valois party, opponents of the Emperor, and the Duke of Guise, whose faction received support from Spain. Romegas seems to have been inclined towards the latter camp, and the fact that he belonged to the Langue of Provence supports this supposition, as the Duke of Guise commanded strong loyalties in the south of France. Romegas was reputed to favour the Spanish knights, while the support given to La Cassière by the Spanish king, Philip II, has been described by contemporary historians as moderate. The dramatic nature of the quarrel is evident in the fact that a Spanish fleet was sent to Malta on the pretext of safeguarding the Grandmaster's life but with secret instructions to lend military assistance to the rebels. Not so moderate was the support of the French king, the Valois Henry III, to La Cassière as his influence in the Papal court was instrumental to having the Grandmaster reinstated in office.

The situation was not eased by the Grandmaster's assiduousness in asserting his authority. The Venerable Council of the Order was no longer called every five years, as was customary, and the holding of sessions was placed at the Grandmaster's discretion. Meanwhile, the French knights were doing their utmost to lever themselves into a position of superiority within the institution and to derive maximum benefit from being in a majority and wielding, as a result, greater financial power.
The exercising of greater autocratic power and unrest among the members of the Order was an unedifying combination, and insubordination grew so rife that there ensued a loosening of the ethic of communality. Indeed, the Convent could not reintroduce the idea of the *collachio*, or the urban space reserved entirely for the Knights, in the new city of Valletta and many members of the Order began to set up their own distinct dwellings.

The Sacra Infirmeria, or the hospital of the Knights, built by Grand Master La Cassiere.

A street in Birgu.

seeking redress in Rome. Pope Gregory XIII (1572-85) acted with some prudence, even if this event served him, to use the words of the American historian Elisabeth Schermerhorn, as 'a pretext for intervention in the private affairs of the Sovereign Order' (Schermerhorn, 125). It meant that the Pope was being appointed as arbiter and his superiority was being recognised. For the papacy, indeed, the silver lining in this unedifying business was the implicit recognition of Papal authority and the upholding of Catholic values in Christian states.

Insistence by La Cassière on observation of the Convent's rules provoked a revolt. The Grandmaster was imprisoned and Romegas was elected lieutenant. Any attempts at compromise failed.
Some knights wanted to free La Cassière but the only feasible solution lay in

Grandmaster Jean de la Cassiere. Saint John's Co-Cathedral Museum, Valletta.

On the instigation of Henry III, once the Grandmaster reached Rome he was received by the Pope with all the honours befitting his rank, while Romegas was given a cool reception. Antagonism between both sides persisted in Rome, to the extent that brawls between the parties erupted in St Peter's square. The Pope decreed that La Cassière was to be reinstated.
This vindicated La Cassière but did nothing to resolve deeper problems. The death of the major players in Rome was what brought temporary harmony within the Order.
The next Grandmasters could make use of an important trump card in keeping the brethren occupied: namely the constant threat of a new Turkish invasion, hence constraining many within the Order to re-focus energy and money on an on-going programme of fortification and defence. It was a programme that was destined to last until the last decade of the Hospitallers' stay in Malta.

The Maltese Citadel

Portrait of Grandmaster Verdale wearing a cardinal's hat.

Chapter 8

La Cassière's successor, Fra Hugues Loubex de Verdale, committed the Order to new structures of defence. The building of fortifications had a dual function. First they were intended to block invasions from the outside. The second function, which is less well known, was to apply internal control over the population living within walled cities through the posting of garrisons in key areas of the defence system. In Europe, this created general bitterness and popular resentment towards the building of forts within the cities' parameters throughout the late medieval period. Malta was not an exception and in the fifteenth century the Maltese *Universitas,* or the governing body of Mdina, had striven hard to remove a fortification tower from inside the city. By the end of the sixteenth century, a general change occurred in the mentality of people throughout Europe regarding defence strategies. The feature of having towers and fortifications incorporated within the city's walls began to be generally accepted and Malta was again not an exception. Verdale found no popular resistance to having two towers added to the entrance of the city (known today as the cavalier of St James and St John) for a better defence of the gates, even though cannons could easily be turned onto the city in case of an insurrection.

Verdale was one of the first Grandmasters in Malta to visibly and publicly mix leisure with defence. Some small rooms built by La Valette as hunting lodges at the *Boschetto* woods in the limits of Rabat were upgraded into a fortified castle to serve as his and his successors' country residence. The next Grandmaster, Martino Garzes, would seek to strengthen the defences by ordering the building of a number of coastal towers at vantage points on the coast. In Gozo, he strengthened the fortifications of the sole fortified town on this island, the *Cittadella*, and built another coastal tower at Mgarr.

The threat of another siege continued to haunt the Order and at the beginning of the seventeenth century another Turkish invasion appeared plausible. Once again, the response focused on strengthening the island's coastal defence system. Grandmaster Alof de Wignacourt (1601-1622) erected a tower at the northern part of the island, precisely at St Paul's Bay, in 1609, while a bigger fort, named San Luciano at Marsaxlokk, was built in 1610. Such a large scale military development was not in vain. In 1614, the Turkish Armada was actually sighted off Malta, but fears of a siege receded when the engagement only took the form of a half-day raid on the southern part of the island.

A contemporary eyewitness recorded that 'It was Sunday, 6 July 1614, when the Turkish Armada made up of sixty galleys came and disembarked at Wed il hain [Wied il-Ghajn] and raided Zejtun. But by Divine Grace, they captured no one, except for an unfortunate man, who was taken into slavery while seeking refuge. The Turks pillaged many houses, and caused great damage to the Church of Saint Catherine (Zejtun) and burned

Grandmaster Martin Garzes (1595-1601). Wignacourt Museum, Rabat.

large number of fields'(Gudja Baptismal Register, Vol.1. f.637).

The reaction of the Order was predictable. Wignacourt ordered the building of three coastal towers at the southern end of Malta. The first was at St Thomas Bay, where the armada had landed. Its construction started in that same year of the attack. The second coastal tower was at Xghajra, situated half way between Gallows Point and Marsascala. The latter was intended for the defence of the people of Zabbar and Bormla. Wignacourt also projected the construction of a tower for the defence of the island of Comino. However, this did not materialise and it was left to his successor, the Basque Antoine De Paule, to undertake that project.

Grandmaster De Paule's ambitions far exceeded this tower, and his far-reaching plans envisaged the building of a new fortified suburb in the hinterland of Valletta. He brought to Malta the engineer Pietro Paolo Floriani to supervise the construction of a new line of fortifications, which was aimed at disciplining the urban chaos in the area presently known as Floriana by imposing a grid structure supported by outer bastions. The work was completed during the office of De Paule's successors Jean Paul Lascaris Castellar in 1650. Lascaris Castellar also set out to fortify the opposing flank of Valletta, the emerging town of Bormla. A new line of defence was proposed for Bormla, which came to be known as the Firenzuola lines – after the architect Vincenzo Maculano da Firenzuola, who undertook the design of these bastions. These walls were intended to defend Galley Creek, the neck of water between Birgu and Senglea, from land attack from the hinterland of Bormla. It was also during Lascaris Castellar's time that six new coastal towers were

Wignacourt's Tower built to protect Saint Paul's Bay.

Grandmaster Martin De Redin's portrait. Wignacourt Museum, Rabat.

constructed. This effort was consolidated by the next Grandmaster, Martin de Redin, who added thirteen towers, raising their number to nineteen, and strengthened the fortifications of Mdina.

After the loss of Venetian Crete to the Turks in 1669, the Order had ample reason to conclude that Malta might be the next Ottoman target. To counter this eventuality, the military engineer of the Duke of Savoy, Count Maurizio Valperga, was invited to Malta to assess the fortifications on the island. Among other measures, he suggested the building of a belt of bastions that stretched from Birgu, went around Bormla and reached up to Senglea. This belt would come to be known as the Cottonera lines. There was no let up in the military programme and in 1670 the last unsecured peninsula of the Grand Harbour, situated at the harbour's entrance, was fortified. The new fort was named Ricasoli after its benefactor, the Knight Giovanni Francesco Ricasoli, donated 20,000 scudi for its building.

In the middle of the eighteenth century, a new fortress city was planned for Gozo: Fort Chambray. Again, it was named after the knight who donated much of the money for its construction. However, only the outer lines of fortifications were built, for the fort remained unpopulated.

In the early eighteenth century further projects were undertaken under the direction of the French architect, Charles

A coastal tower.

François de Mondion who reinforced the fortification networks on the outskirts of Valletta by adding a new gate, known as Porte des Bombes. Before this project was completed, Grandmaster Antonio Manoel de Vilhena sought to overturn what he considered a superannuated policy of fortification building by a more forward-looking programme. This was based on the effort to reach a peaceful coexistence with North African States through an armistice with the Turks. However, by the 1720s, all efforts failed and this option had to be discarded. Grandmaster de Vilhena returned to the old option of military planning and boasted, by means of the inscription he commissioned for the new gates of Porte des Bombes, that 'while the Turks wage battles everywhere, the Maltese behind these city's walls feel secure'. Security was also strengthened in the other harbour cities of Birgu, Bormla and Senglea by continuing the works on the Cottonera lines, which had been only half finished at the death of Grandmaster Nicola Cottoner. In addition, De Vilhena reinforced the entrance of Mdina's bastions. He also undertook the building of a new fort on a deserted islet in the middle of Marsamxett harbour. Eventually, the islet was named after him: Manoel Island. All these works involved enormous capital expenditure on the part of the Knights. The island appeared almost impregnable. Only minor areas of the coast were left undefended. It is to be expected that the strengthening of the island's defences would have proceeded only fitfully after de

Another coastal tower.

One of the gates built along the new lines of Fortifications known as the Cottonera Lines. The gate is adorned by a bronze bust of Grandmaster Nicola Cottoner, who was the sponsor of this project.

Vilhena's death. Besides pressing financial pressures brought about by the enormous debts created by these massive building projects, the island was hit by an economic recession resulting from a general decline in trade all over the Mediterranean world. Lack of liquidity meant that the Order was faced with the difficulty of providing garrisons for all these fortifications: in other words, it did not have enough soldiers on its payroll for the defence of the forts. In 1775, a small group of local priests, exasperated by the despotic manner in which the Grandmasters dictated matters in Malta, planned a revolt and without great difficulty succeeded in occupying Fort Saint Elmo and the tower of Saint James in Valletta. This revolt exposed the lack of resources and the vulnerability of the Order's defences in the face of a determined and well-executed attack. In addition, the upkeep of the fortifications was becoming prohibitive. Consequently, by the later part of the eighteenth century, more cost-efficient modes of defence were resorted to. Especially worthy of note is the reliance on the *fougasse*, a hole in the ground dug at an angle and filled with stones and ordnance material that could then be fired onto enemy ships.

There was one last fort, however, which was projected at Sliema point towards the end of the Order's rule in Malta. It

Grandmaster Nicola Cottoner (1663-1680). Saint John's Co-Cathedral Museum.

The main gate of Fort Ricasoli.

Porte des Bombes. The gate on the right was built by Grandmaster Vilhena. The other gate was added in the nineteenth century by the British.

was financed by a knight of the Order, the Bailiff René Jacques de Tigné, and its construction reflected new military realities. It had low bastions while the defensive mechanisms, such as the carriages for the cannons, were entrenched below ground level. It was designed to counter new strategies in artillery which made high walls easy targets for enemy fire and unfit to resist the power of the new cannon balls. Its place at the entrance of the harbour, flanking Fort Saint Elmo, reflected the need for a new type of military defence at the island's most strategic point. However, as the events of 1798 would clearly show, all these defence mechanisms proved futile for an aristocratic Order which had lost by the end of the eighteenth century, all traces of a nostalgic chivalric past. To make matters worse, members began to be lured towards revolutionary ideals and began to sympathise with Napoleon Bonaparte.

Chapter 9

Naval Engagements in a Closed Sea

The massive fortification of Malta proceeded against a backdrop of continuous naval incursions by the Knights upon the Turks. Following the death of Suleiman the Magnificent, hostilities tended to concentrate increasingly on engagements at sea, with corsairing by both parties reaching unprecedented heights. The first major encounter between the Christian and Ottoman fleets occurred in 1571, six years after the siege of Malta, off the coast of Lepanto in the Ionian Sea. The Hospitallers sent their galleys in support of the Christian armada which had been assigned to the defence of Cyprus. The vessels of the Order were far from being the most numerous in the coalition, especially as during the previous year it had suffered a serious defeat when three of its four galleys were captured by the Turkish Admiral El Louck Ali Fartax, now governor of Algiers and a veteran of the siege of Malta. Among the captured vessels, there was the Order's flagship, whose pilot was the Maltese siege hero, Orlando Magro. It was such a humiliating defeat for the Knights that Magri and the Hospitaller in charge of the overall squadron, Francois de Saint Clement, were brought to Malta in chains and sentenced to death by hanging.

The battle of Lepanto therefore represented an opportunity for the Knights to recapture some honour. Their performance, however, was poor. They were given the privilege of being placed on the right of the Christian flagship. The right flank was put under the overall command of the Genoese admiral Giovanni Andrea Doria, while the head of the Christian army was Don John of Austria, half-brother with Philip II, and son of Charles V. At first, the naval battle looked grim for the Christian forces. The Turks succeeded in making good gains in the morning, reaping the advantage of sailing with the winds in their favour. The Hospitallers' three galleys came under the direct fire of the Algerian seaman, Ali el-Uluji. He directed his fleet into a frontal attack on the Knights' vessels, causing great havoc to the extent that the Hospitaller flagship, the *galera capitana,* was captured. Then, at noon, the wind changed direction, and compelled changes in strategy on both sides. With the winds now in their favour, it became easier for the Christians to strike for victory. The Christian ships helped the Order to recapture the lost flagship and even more importantly allowed Andrea Doria to break the front line of the Turkish fleet and wreak devastation, so that by sunset the Christian fleet was victorious.
The battle was marked by bad seamanship on both sides. Division within the

A painting representing the battle of Lepanto. Notice that the Ottoman fleet is shown being supported by small devils painted next to the mast of the Ottoman galleys. Maritime Museum, Birgu.

The Admiral Andrea Doria, embodied in the figure of Neptune. Presidential Palace, Valletta.

A model of a galley. Maritime Museum, Birgu.

command of the Christian forces was counter-balanced by inexperience among the Turkish admirals, and this was probably the major factor in their defeat. However, the Christians were unable to follow up the victory. Political division in Europe, where most of the Christian states sought to consolidate their boundaries rather than engage in a Mediterranean war with the Sublime Porte, allowed the Turks time to regroup. More importantly, the aim for which the battle was fought, the return of Cyprus to Venice, was not achieved. Cyprus remained in Turkish hands, inducing Ferdinand Braudel to remark that Lepanto was one of those 'victories that led nowhere' (Braudel, 1106). Within a year they had rebuilt their fleet and continued to expand their activities in the Mediterranean without encountering real opposition. The conquest of Candia (modern Crete) in 1669 is a clear example that the Turkish might had not abated since 1571 and Ottoman decline was still remote. With the East increasingly under Ottoman control, and with a new navy entering the equation, the war at sea would escalate in the decades to come.

In fact, the Battle of Lepanto can be taken as a warning of further wars between the cross and the crescent, as the naval engagements throughout the seventeenth century between the Christians, assisted by the Knights, and the Turks testify. In 1601, the Knights' ships successfully attacked the fortress of Passavà in Morea (Greece). In that same year, Hammamet in Tunisia was also captured, and a number of inhabitants were herded off to the slave-market. Then, in April 1602, the fortress cities of Patras and Lepanto were taken and their reserves of wheat plundered in order to offset shortages that had hit Malta during that year. During this attack, three Ottoman merchant ships laden with wheat were captured. Moreover, in 1622, the Order's squadron made a successful attack on the fortress of Castel Farnese in Morea.

The war of Candia, which began in 1644, brought unending conflict in the East. It

A model of the hull of a vascello. Maritime Museum, Birgu.

A model of a tartana. Maritime Museum, Birgu.

Uniforms worn by Hospitaller Naval Officers. Maritime Museum, Birgu.

focused on naval engagements between Venice, assisted by the Order, and the Porte. The cause of the conflict was the Hospitallers' corsairing activity and the Venetians' failure to curtail what to the Turks appeared to be blatant piracy. Venice was accused of being in compliance with the Knights by permitting entry to Hospitaller corsairing ships in the harbours of Crete. In such circumstances, Venice could not avoid conflict. The Turks embarked on a long war from which no respite occurred until the island fell utterly into their hands in 1669. This event did not dissuade the Hospitallers from continuing their warfare on the borders of the Ottoman Empire. On the contrary, it forced the Venetians to seek the alliance of the Hospitaller knights in their expeditions against the Turks. In 1687, the Knights' galleys sided with Venice in the conquest of Morea, and in 1689 Hospitallers were part of the Christian Imperial army that marched over to retake Belgrade.

The Order's biggest success during this period was in fact the assistance given to the Venetians in the occupation of Morea. The expedition began with the successful military endeavours of 1687. In that year Navarino, Modone, Patras, Lepanto, Corinth and Athens were occupied. Then in 1689 came the conquest of Morea, which was followed by naval raids on the Ionian cities of Santa Maura and Prevesa, while the island of Chios was temporarily occupied. The eventual occupation of Morea would render it necessary for the Christian forces to alter their policy to one of consolidation. In 1704, the galleys of the Order were part of a squadron made up of a bigger armada constituted by Venice, the papacy and the Holy League in a last successful attempt to save Morea

A naval battle that took place on 3 May 1706 in which the Hospitaller galleys captured the flagship of the Tunisian fleet. Maritime Museum, Birgu.

for the Venetian *Serenissima*.
This war in Morea was the last opportunity for Venice to show to the other European powers of the time that it had its place in the international scene. The Venetian domination had a mixed reaction in Athens. Some Athenians supported the Venetians, who were seen as liberators, but others preferred to support Turkey. The patriarch of Constantinople was constrained by the Ottomans to force Athens to support the Turks. Since the Orthodox Church showed opposition, the future of the Venetians was grim. The Turkish reaction to recover what was considered in Constantinople as a lost territory was to be expected, and it occurred in 1715, when after a short siege the whole of Morea returned to the fold of the Ottoman Empire. But if military activities on land were glorious events for the Turks, they were to experience different fortunes at sea. War at sea continued to swing in the Knights' favour, with victories throughout the eighteenth century. At the opening of the eighteenth century, the Knights participated in the attack on Oran in Algiers and they captured among other prizes the Tripolitan flagship in 1706. In 1709, it was the turn of the flagship of Algiers to fall prey to the Hospitallers' fleet. Then, during the reign of Grandmaster Ramon Perellos y Roccaful, the galley squadron was given a facelift by the introduction of four new ships-of-the-line carrying 56 guns each.

Though corsairs lost some of their seventeenth-century eminence, exploits were still current since good yields were still forthcoming. Fra Jacques de Chambray sailed on 31 caravans between 1723 and 1749, roaming and raiding the Levant. Fra Pierre-Andre de Suffren de Saint-Tropez, after gaining experience in the Hospitaller's seafaring expeditions in the Levant, fought on behalf of the French against the British in the American war of Independence. Under his command, the French navy struck decisive victories in the Indian Ocean. Probably the last important naval engagement for the Knights came in 1784, when their navy assisted Portuguese ships in shelling the city of Algiers, the haven of Muslim corsairs.

Portrait of Grandmaster Perellos.

The Artistic Heritage

Chapter 10

A general consensus exists among historians that the arrival of the Order of St John in 1530 changed forever the political, social and economic character of the small community in Malta. The Knights proceeded to dismantle Malta's medieval structures and plunged the island into the late Renaissance world. A sixteenth-century traveller, Nicola de Nicolay, noticed as early as 1551 the Knights' inclinations towards the arts and the pursuit of life's pleasures. The peninsula opposite to Birgu was changed into a hunting paradise by the reigning Grandmaster, d'Homedes. On this land, he built a palace and a big garden which, according to Nicolay, had a variety of fruit trees such as prunes, pears, common figs, prickly pears and other fruits besides herbs 'of incomparable goodness' (de Nicolay, 37). Grandmaster La Valette initiated a similar project when he transformed a small garden next to Rabat into a small wood by planting a number of trees. Appropriately, he called the place, where he could practise his hunting hobby in tranquillity, 'Boschetto'.

The Hospitallers' interests in aesthetic matters were given a boost just after the siege. Before 1565 most of the and employed by Grandmaster Verdale on works both at his palace in Valetta and the newly constructed castle at the Boschetto.

A decade later, the most significant episode in the Knights' patronage of the arts occurred when they employed Michelangelo Merisi da Caravaggio (1573-1610). Caravaggio came to Malta as an outlaw. He was involved in a murder in Italy and to avoid imprisonment or capital punishment he escaped to Naples and from there to Malta, where he gained employment with the Order and was awarded a Hospitaller's habit for his services. He remained on the island for fifteen months and painted some of his masterpieces during that time, including the beheading of St John the Baptist for the Oratory of Saint John's Church in Valletta, the portrait of the Grandmaster Alof de Wignacourt (now at the Louvre), St Jerome (now at Saint John's Co-cathedral), a painting of Saint Mary Magdalen and another portrait of Wignacourt. These latter two paintings are now lost. The stay of this master of the *chiaroscuro* came to an abrupt end following his involvement in a brawl in which swords were quickly unsheathed. He was defrocked and imprisoned, but

The castle built by Grandmaster Verdale at the Boschetto Gardens.

The beheading of Saint John the Baptist by Michelangelo Merisi da Caravaggio. Saint John's Co-Cathedral Museum, Valletta.

Portrait of Grandmaster Alof de Wignacourt. It was painted by Giulio Cassarino and considered to be an original copy of a lost painting by Michelangelo Merisi da Caravaggio. Wignacourt Museum, Rabat.

appears to have had some influential friends who aided his escape from prison, after which he secured a passage to Naples.

The arts in Malta would experience new trends during the reign of De Paule. Following the Venetian custom whereby patricians began to build their country villas on the *Terraferma*, de Paule commissioned the building of two grandiose palaces: one at Attard, named San Anton after his patron saint, and the other at Paola. San Anton survives today as the official residence of the President of the Republic of Malta. The palace at Paola, together with its enormous gardens, was destroyed in the nineteenth century to make way for an industrial zone. At Paola, the Grandmaster's palace was part of a larger design of development of the area. It formed part of a new town that the Grandmaster wanted to develop on the outskirts of the harbour cities of Birgu and Senglea. The place included a new church dedicated to one of the Hospitallers' medieval saints, Ubaldesca, as well as extensive stables and a hunting lodge.

The next painter of international repute to work in Malta was Mattea Preti. The *Calabrese*, as Preti was often referred in acknowledgement of his origins from the town of Taverna in Calabria, was responsible for most of the paintings and decorations of the Conventual Church of Saint John. Indeed it could be said that the true artistic renaissance in Malta began during the reign of the two Cottoner brothers, Raphael and Nicola. It was thanks to their efforts and patronage that

St. Magdalene by Cassarino. It is also considered to be an authentic copy of another lost painting by Michelangelo Merisi da Caravaggio. Wignacourt Museum, Rabat.

The façade of the Hospitallers' Conventual Church of Saint John, Valletta.

Preti completed the ceiling and many of the side chapels with other works of art.

Malta continued to host renowned artists in the following century. Between 1680 and 1738, Malta benefited from the services of one of the most important Roman architects of the period, Romano Carapecchia, who was responsible for the design of a number of churches in Valletta and the relining of a number of Church facades in the Roman Baroque idiom. Probably his most important secular building in Malta was the Manoel Theatre. Another architect working in Malta at the time was Carlo Gimach, who

The interior of Saint John's Conventual Church.

The Penitent Saint Peter, by Mattia Preti (1613-1699). Wignacourt Museum, Rabat.

like Carapecchia had studied in Rome. He designed a number of important buildings, the foremost being the Auberge of Bavaria in Valletta.

Further artistic treasures were acquired by the conventual church of Saint John after the election of Ramon Perellos y Roccaful to the magistracy of the Order. Perellos commissioned a set of tapestries for the conventual church of Saint John from Flanders and another set for his palace from the Gobelins factory of Paris. Most of the former tapestries were executed on designs of Peter Paul Rubens. The only two tapestries that did not follow Rubens' drawings were executed on sketches by Nicholas Poussin and Mattia Preti. The tapestries depict episodes from the life of Christ and the Counter-Reformation. Another set of tapestries was commissioned for the hall where the Grand Council, or the governing body of the Order, held its meetings. The scenes of the latter are secular and exotic, and depicted hunting scenes, and wildlife and exotic fruits from Latin American islands of the Caribbean.

The eighteenth century continued to witness the spread of Baroque architecture in Malta. In the 1720s, Grandmaster De Vilhena sought the services of the French engineer Francois de Mondion, who was given the portfolio for the reorganisation of the urban fabric of Floriana. The same architect was entrusted with the design of a new entrance to Mdina as well as the building of a new magisterial palace at the entrance of this old capital of Malta. According to prevalent fashion, the baroque idiom employed on the buildings expressed ideas of political absolutism. In other words, the endogenous elite, still considering Mdina as the seat of their lost medieval power, were reminded, through the regimented and articulated designs of the palace façade of the absolute powers, of the ruling prince in Malta.

The taste for rococo grandeur first became evident during Grandmaster Pinto's reign, and architecture, as a medium for the expression of political despotism reached its apex through the relining and expansion of the Grandmaster's palace in Valletta. Two magnificent doors were added to the building and long enclosed

The interior of the Manoel Theatre.

Opposite, a Caribbean scene from one of the tapestries ordered for the Grandmaster's palace. Presidential Palace, Valletta.

A cabreo *with scenes of Galley Greek in Senglea. National Library, Valletta.*

conducted through Greek intermediaries living in Christian territories. In practice, the prospect of a share of the profits, especially those accruing from the consignment of timber to the island, led to some startling situations. It is reported that 'several Greek vessels proceeded to Malta under cover of the flag of Jerusalem, at times disguising themselves as Venetian subjects from Cephalonia, but the moment they left the harbour of Valletta or Marsamxett, they would hoist the Turkish emblem' (Mallia-Milanes 1992, 226-7).

Religious processions were a common feature in Early Modern Malta. The Inquisitor's Palace, Birgu.

The importance of this Greek community was recognised by European merchants, particularly the French, who more than once in the eighteenth century availed themselves of their skills by appointing them their agents in the importation of grain from the East. Through the use of these channels, eighteenth-century Malta was importing grain from mainland Turkey.

De Nicolay's portrait of a sixteenth century Maltese courtesan. National Library, Valletta.

It is not difficult to understand, especially in the years 1587-92 or the first decade of the seventeenth century when famine ravaged the island, why the Order resorted to corsairing activity. Under a distortion of the nineteenth-century romantic view, the rural areas were assigned by various contemporary historians an economic potential which they never had, namely that of being able to provide work and food for a hungry population. Poverty and famine was wrongly regarded as an urban phenomenon. Some Romantic visionaries even argued that the urban poor should be sent to the countryside, where there was enough land to provide work and produce to overcome urban famine. Yet, historical records portray a different reality. Neither the indigent nor the labouring poor found the desired economic support in the rural areas, as the Romantics had wrongly anticipated. One can immediately understand why the Maltese towns, first Birgu and later Valletta, assumed importance not only through new job opportunities offered to both the local and foreign workers, but also to the poor and even the beggars. The towns afforded refuge and the hope of food, as well as alms.

Indeed, many foreign travellers to Malta noticed that behind the prosperity of some lay a more general social wretchedness. The contact with the Levant, for example, left its marks from the early decades of the Knights' stay in Malta. The traveller Nicola de Nicolay found much oriental flavour in Hospitaller Birgu, in 1551. The city was described by Nicholay as adorned with Greek and Latin churches, but their presence was not enough to deter the development and expansion of prostitution. The presence of Knights from different parts of Europe attracted a number of courtesans of different ethnic origin, such as Greeks, Italians, Spanish, Moors, as well as Maltese. The Maltese appeared rather rustic in outlook. The women were said 'to wear only one dress in summer, consisting of a long shirt of white cloth, which was tied by a girdle under the breasts, and covered their head by a long mantel of white thin wool called by the Moors "barnuco". The textile fabric used in summer was so thin as to make all the curves of their body transparent to the onlookers' (De Nicholay, 35).

In the early seventeenth century, Captain Alonso de Contreras, a Spanish privateer who used Malta as a base, recounted how he divided his booty between gifts for Our Lady of Grace venerated at the Zabbar parish Church and his *quiraca* or courtesan. In the middle of the seventeenth century, the English traveller, Philip Skippon, spoke disparagingly of morality in the Maltese harbour towns, and went further in describing the female population as 'infamous' (Skippon, 623). George Sandys would elaborate in greater detail on the conduct of some of the women of low repute. He explained that the practice of prostitution in Malta was passed from mother to daughter and recounted that mothers accompanied their young females in prostitution, literally serving as their pimps. Ships were approached by prostitutes accompanied by their mothers and once within sight of the sailors, the daughters would instantly strip naked and leap into the sea (Sandys, 177-8). Sandys sarcastically remarked that in Valletta there were three nunneries: one for the virgins, another for penitent whores and the third for their bastard offspring. (Sandys, 182).

In travellers' accounts and some European literature, the Hospitallers themselves were becoming associated with licentiousness. In his short novel *Candide*, Voltaire accused the Knights of immorality, ascribing to them, perhaps wrongly, the habit of denuding their captured victims in their avid search for jewels. Captured travellers, in particular women, were stripped naked by the Maltese crew at the service of the Knights, for their clothing and belongings formed part of the latter's booty, together with any jewels or gold that the travellers would have hidden on their person. These strip searches, admits Voltaire, were so widespread as to become 'one of those international laws which', he says, 'had never been questioned'. (Chapter 11).

Accusations of immorality continued to dog the Hospitallers even after their expulsion from the island. The loss of Malta allowed greater freedom to the island's inhabitants to discuss matters that had been previously taboo more openly. Decadence turned out to be a convenient scapegoat in some accounts of the Order's loss of Malta. Some Knights expressed dismay at the shameless profligacy and dissipation of certain brethren and prostitutes were blamed for the destruction of the Knights' chivalric virtues. They began to point their finger at some of their fellow brothers and accuse them of tyrannical behaviour whenever they forced young or married females to sexual outrages. For instance the secretary of the last Grandmaster, Pierre Jean Louis Ovide Doublet, who incidentally defected to the French force in the takeover of the island,-claimed in his memoirs that the knights 'made no secrets of keeping mistresses, generally married women and mothers of families, a practice which became so general, that neither age nor ministers of the Gospel, dissolute like the rest, blushed at the fact.' Doublet added that there were well known instances of serious sexual harassment. A Maltese man married to an attractive woman risked unjustifiable exile for no reason other than having his wife engaged in the service of a lascivious knight. These cases, insists Doublet, were not frequent, but the Order's reputation was not helped by its failure to discipline its members. The English poet Samuel Taylor Coleridge, who in the first decade of the nineteenth century served as secretary to the Civil Commissioner in Malta, Alexander Ball, had a similar story to tell. He recounts how 'every knight attached himself to some family as their patron and friend, and to him the honour of a sister, or a daughter, was sacrificed as a matter of course' (Coleridge, 152).

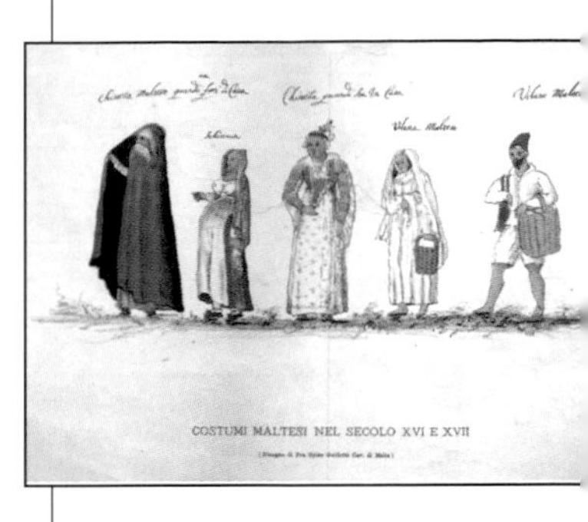

The different Maltese social strata at the turn of the seventeenth century. National Library, Valletta.

A seventeenth-century painting of Saint John's Church in Valletta with city gentry in the foreground. Museum of Fine Arts, Valletta.

The Hospitallers' ethic obliged them to desist from such activities, especially following the Reformation ideals when chastity gained an increasingly important value among religious institutions. Transgressors, however, were not easily controllable. Indeed, though the early laws prescribed banishment from the island for such members, enforcement of the law was rare. Regulations against loitering in Valletta were undermined by the large number of prostitutes in the city. In 1631 the policy was relaxed in the hope of more realistic effectiveness: prostitutes were now simply prohibited from living in the main and principal streets of the town. But as the above quotations of foreign witnesses demonstrate, prostitutes were soon to return to their normal activities, to continue practising their trade in Valletta practically unhindered up to contemporary times.

Portrait of an eighteenth-century priest. Wignacourt Museum, Rabat.

The Question of Sovereignty

Chapter 12

Charles V's grant of Malta to the Knights in 1530 seriously compromised any hopes for sovereignty. Some sections of the Order considered the terms offered by Charles as a hindrance to the pursuit of rights for autonomous existence. In the preliminary negotiations, Charles denied the Hospitallers the right to mint coins and he continued to regard Malta and Tripoli as an extension of the territory, over which he had full judicial control. These terms were increasingly resisted by French members of the Order, who resented the curtailment of independence and the implied subjection to the Habsburg Empire. Indeed, their loyalty to the French King, Francis I, made any prospect of obedience to Spain and the Emperor undesirable. Consequently the Grandmaster of the time, L'Isle Adam, was forced to seek some form of compromise between the terms of the Emperor's dispensation and the French knights' ambivalence over the terms of the agreement. It was decided that Malta would only be enfeoffed to the Knights, and in recognition the Knights were to give a falcon to the Emperor each year. In return, the Order obtained the right to mint its own money, the authority to appoint ambassadors to Christian states and the wielding of inalienable rights over Malta. The Emperor accepted that the Knights were to become *de facto* princes on the granted lands. Nevertheless, the power was soon to be challenged by the new sixteenth-century magnate corporations.

The setting up of the tribunal of the Roman Inquisition in Malta was in part an infringement of the medieval ideal of princely rule. However, the inquisition was only one aspect of a bigger movement engulfing the Roman Church and threatening the Order's autonomy. The upheaval caused by Martin Luther in 1518 brought a belated reaction in the Church, resulting in the Council of Trent's ordinances and Counter Reformation measures, which led to the revival of apostolic visits, besides the setting up of the herein mentioned corporation of the Roman Inquisition. In 1575, the Order reluctantly accepted that the Papal delegate, Mgr. Pietro Dusina, should make an apostolic visit to the island. A similar situation had occurred in Italy, where in Milan Bishop Carlo Borromeo enforced upon the Hospitallers' commanders his right to enter and visit them as part of the general visit of ecclesiastical properties within his diocese. In Malta, Dusina's visit led to the establishment of a permanent court of the Inquisition, which not only infringed the religious liberties of the Maltese but also those of the Knights. The Order, as an approved institution of the Church, could not oppose the setting up of the tribunal. The Inquisitor was considered as the Papal representative in Malta, and the Knights, in their capacity as monks, owed their allegiance to the papacy. The Inquisition's stay in Malta was sullied by a number of quarrels between the tribunal of the Inquisition and the Hospitallers, and personally between the Inquisitor and the Grandmaster. The only concession made by the Inquisition was in the formation of the tribunal for the Knights. All the Hospitallers were liable to prosecution but the Holy Office accepted that the Knights should be subjected to a special trial, in which representatives of the Order were allowed to sit with the Inquisitor on the board of inquiry.

Once this conflict was quelled, a new threat loomed. This time, the challenge was secular in nature. The changes that began to affect the internal organisation of the Spanish Kingdom, together with the propagation of the new political ideas in Italy and France, undermined part of the Hospitallers' claims on the sovereignty over the island of Malta. In the age of the Enlightenment, a new concept of statehood began to take shape in Europe, which required that States should have a fixed geographical boundary that contained a coherent ethnic identity. Eighteenth-century Grandmasters began to play with this new idea, to the extent of incorporating it in their political strategy. Malta was an island with no geopolitical problems. The ultimate objective was to

A Hospitaller silver coin minted during the time of Grandmaster Despuig. Wignacourt Museum, Rabat.

gain more autonomy that would eventually lead the Order to have its own sovereign land, without incurring any allegiance to the Spanish or Neapolitan monarchies.

The origins of this new political scenario lies in the Treaty of Westphalia in 1648, in which the international community affirmed most of the present-day European boundaries while the figure of the monarch was declared to be above all professed beliefs. In other words, Westphalia sanctioned the religious division in Europe and recognised the mutual existence of both Protestant and Catholic States. The recognition of the existence of Protestant States by the staunch Catholic countries shows that the north was holding the upper hand both politically and economically, while the traditional powers in the Mediterranean were slowly declining to the benefit of England and France. Spain lost much of its past power, as did Holland, while the Turkish Empire had reached the limits of its expansion and fell back to safeguard its possessions. Hospitaller Malta was caught in the struggle for supremacy between England and France. Despite the fact that England was no longer within the folds of the Catholic Church, the Order would still show respect to this Protestant power by adopting a neutral stand in its wars. In certain respects this affected the destiny of Malta, as the Order failed to seize the opportunity to move towards total sovereignty.

The occasion came in 1700, when the nephew of Louis XIV of France became king of Spain, as Philip V, with full approval from France. This was interpreted by other European powers, in particular England and the Netherlands, as a sign of the impending political unity between France and Spain, and Europe was soon driven into a new war. The Order recognised Philip V as the new king, and this meant acknowledgement of his role as Malta's ultimate sovereign. In the resulting Treaty of Utrecht in 1713, Sicily was given to Amadeo II of Savoy, who recognised the *tratte* privileges (the tax-free importation of cereals from Sicily) of Malta, but at the same time the islands were declared to be neutral territories. One wonders why the Grandmaster of the day, the Spanish Ramon Perellos y Roccafull, was inclined to acknowledge Amadeo. Was it a result of fear of international pressure by the big powers, or was it the case that the great economic dependence on Sicily forced the Grandmaster's hand not to take a real political stand on the matter in order to avoid the question of total independence which could have endangered the economic existence of Malta? It could also be that Perellos had no ambition towards full sovereignty.

The reverse of two silver coins. The first one was minted during the reign of Grand Master Perellos. It only carries an open crown. The second one was minted during the reign of Grand Master Pinto. It portrays the image of a closed crown. Wignacourt Museum, Rabat.

Whatever the case, the international situation was further complicated in 1718, when Spain sought a revision of the Treaty of Utrecht by invading Sicily. This political move went against British interests in the region, which were clearly expressed in the heightening of British presence in the central Mediterranean and in the support given to the Kingdom of Savoy. Two years later, a compromise was reached. Sicily was retained by Spain but in return, Spain ceded Sardinia to Savoy. Once again the Order of Saint John, well aware of its limited sway over European politics, upheld the reaffirmation of the Utrecht Treaty and recognised Spain's claim on Malta.

The Order's effort to acquire the privileges of statehood was repeated two decades later, but the outcome confirmed the Knights' comparative weakness.

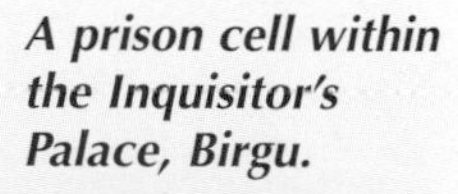

A prison cell within the Inquisitor's Palace, Birgu.

A detail from a survey sheet of a land belonging to the Hospitaller Order, which still shows the escutcheon of Grandmaster Pinto capped by an open crown. Soon this escutcheon would be changed in favour of the closed crown. National Library, Valletta.

Grand Master Vilhena's bronze Monument.

The Hospitallers had limited clout on the diplomatic level. The War of the Polish Succession between 1733 and 1738 opened a new political scenario in Europe, with repercussions reaching the Mediterranean. In this conflict, old enemies forged new alliances. Savoy allied itself with France and Spain against its new enemies, Austria and Russia. The resulting peace treaty created a new monarchy. Naples and Sicily were joined together to form a new kingdom, and Charles VII, son of the Spanish King Philip V, was anointed as the first Bourbon king of the Two Sicilies. This war demonstrated to Grandmaster de Vilhena the weakness of the Order in the face of unrest in European politics. He initially closed Malta's ports to all European powers, but was forced through diplomatic pressure by the same powers to overturn his policy and accept their ships. More importantly, de Vilhena recognised Philip's son as the new king of Malta whereby the Order had lost another chance to achieve full sovereignty over the islands.

The succeeding Grandmaster, Ramon Despuig, was determined to press the Order's claims for sovereignty and when unexpectedly the Bey of Tunis requested the Order's assistance in suppressing a house rebellion by Muslim corsairs, under the excuse that this rebellion could cause damage to Christian commerce, Despuig sent his navy to the region and had the Bey reinstated. As result, the symbols of stately recognition were conferred upon Despuig by the Bey who, once reinstated, paid an official visit to the Grandmaster in Malta, where he was received by the Knights with all the honours associated with figures of state.

Yet, the concept of sovereignty as it is now understood was most actively pursued in Grandmaster Pinto's reign. He arrogated to himself the title of "Eminent Highness", which was exclusive to kings, and adopted the closed crown on his escutcheon. He was careful, maybe out of religious prudence (for as a monk he had professed the vow of poverty), not to be portrayed wearing a crown when sitting for his official portraits. Instead, he preferred to have himself depicted with his finger pointing at the crown, a gesture interpretable as an expression of sovereignty. A different attitude was brought to bear in the minting of coins. Here any constitutional constraints were ignored and the closed crown was embossed on the back of all the coins, in the same way as it was superimposed on each and every escutcheon of Grandmaster Pinto that was affixed onto public and private buildings. Even liturgical vestments did not escape Pinto's concern for the manifestation of his worldly power; they began to be embroidered with the image of a closed crown.

More tangibly, Pinto also sought to acquire the island of Corsica from Genoa. Had he met with success, the Order would have been subjugating another territory to its rule, thus bringing the Hospitaller Institution on a par with the great powers of Europe, in particular France, England, Prussia, Austria and Russia, which at this time were avidly seeking to acquire territories all over the world. Without any doubt, Corsica would have strengthened Pinto's claim to sovereignty, as he would have gained economic autonomy from Sicily. However Pinto's plans failed when he faced a higher bidder, the French king Louis XV.

In 1753, the bishop of Syracuse, Monsignor Francesco Testa, inadvertently gave Pinto the opportunity of strengthening his claim on sovereignty. Crassly, Testa insisted on effecting a pastoral visit to Malta on the grounds that

The effigy of the closed crown found itself everywhere; it was also embroidered on religious vestments. Detail from an antependium donated by Pinto to the Grotto of Saint Paul's in Rabat. Wignacourt Museum, Rabat.

The interior of the Jesuit Church in Valletta.

the island was part of the Two Sicilies. Pinto reacted strongly and, knowing that he commanded the local clergy's support, prohibited Testa from entering Malta by closing the ports to Testa's ship. The king of the Two Sicilies, Charles VII, reacted by halting the *tratte* agreement. This did not intimidate Pinto. He displayed great diplomatic acumen in playing off one big power against another. Overtly, he began discussions with the rival of Charles VII, the king of Savoy, proposing to the latter the importation of wheat from Sardinia. The war of nerves came to an end through a negotiated settlement: Testa agreed not to make the visit, whilst the king's right over the sending of an apostolic visitor was only upheld by Pinto after a prior assurance from the King that he would never make use of such a right.

Pinto used other, more expedient though indirect methods to affirm the Order's sovereignty. The first was to introduce the printing press in Malta. Attempts to do so had been made in the seventeenth century, but had met with failure due to squabbles over censorship. The Bishop and the Inquisitor insisted on sharing with the Grandmaster the right to exercise censorship. The local scene was further marred when in 1642 Rome felt that the prerogative over censorship belonged only to the Inquisitor. Since the Order was not ready to be elbowed out of the control of the press, the project was left to die a natural death. Yet, where Grandmaster Jean Paul Lascaris Castellar had failed, Pinto succeeded. In 1747, Pope Benedict XIV granted the Grandmaster the same rights and prerogatives normally bestowed upon the Inquisitor, leading to the opening of a new printing press in Malta in 1756.

The second incident that earned Pinto international stature concerned the expulsion of the Jesuits. General feelings in Europe over the Jesuit society ran high,

The symbol of the Eucharist. The Jesuits adopted this symbol and prominently displayed it on the façade of their Churches, including the one in Valletta.

An effigy of Saint Ignatius of Loyola on one of the corners of the Jesuit college in Valletta.

not least because it was considered a menace to the concept of statehood. These sentiments would be extensively exploited by the Grandmaster. The Jesuits were widely accused by Enlightenment scholars of diverting the loyalty of their pupils from the monarch to the Pope. In Malta, Pinto created an ambiguous situation where political interests were affected by financial concerns. Pinto excused himself with Rome for having to expel the Jesuits from Malta, arguing that he had to follow similar ordinances that had emanated from Sicily in 1767. Without mentioning the case that Malta was subject to the Sicilian crown, Pinto explained to the Pope that he was following the same policies in force in the kingdom of Spain. In a very polite and elegant manner, he avoided compromising himself over the question of sovereignty, but at the same time foresaw, in furthering his opposition to the Pope, an inevitable humiliation. Thus, he accepted to undertake the advice put forward by the Pope in relation to the Jesuits' property, but at the same time turned the whole affair to his personal advantage from which he himself and his Order could make huge profits. One cannot refrain from noticing that behind the acquisition of the wealth of the Jesuits, Pinto succeeded in partly redeeming the enormous debt of the Order's Treasury, especially if one remembers that his reign was overburdened by spending on paintings and artistic works, which incidentally were aimed at affirming Pinto's false claims on full sovereignty. In this sense, the expulsion of the Jesuits on 22 April 1768 could be viewed as another pawn in Pinto's hand to better finance the herein mentioned claims for sovereignty.

The Order's character as a religious confraternity restricted the Grandmaster's options in dealing with the Jesuit issue. The Holy See intervened in the Jesuits' favour. It may have had to admit defeat in safeguarding the Jesuits' presence in Malta, but it imposed conditions on the use of the property appropriated from the Jesuits. Rome ordered that the assets acquired were to be employed in the people's benefit, and as a result funds were set aside for the establishment of a university. This could appear as a consolidation of the Jesuits' labours in the field of education. Their schools were deeply respected all over Europe, but suspicion of the Jesuits' teaching was what prompted a number of monarchs to press for the Order's expulsion from their territories. In Malta, the Jesuits had been responsible for the opening of a school as early as 1592. However, turning the Jesuits' college in Valletta into a university was in itself an assertion of autonomy for Grandmaster Pinto, as the foundation of universities could only emerge from entities holding the rights of sovereignty. This explains why, throughout their history, universities have sought the approval of Popes or monarchs. Indeed, it is significant that the *Collegium Melitense* (as the Jesuit school in Malta was called) never enjoyed the status of a university, even though it was entitled to confer degrees.

The Order's diplomatic struggle for full sovereignty had unexpected political repercussions on the local elite. The latter were soon influenced by the Hospitallers' political manoeuvres and manipulated them according to their own political needs as, towards the end of the eighteenth century, the wish for some form of self-government began to take root among some of the educated few. The rhetoric of citizenship, a word intimately associated with the values of the enlightenment, became more current. Appeals to the concept of citizenship emanated mostly, as might have been predictable, from a particular class: the bourgeoisie, especially those individuals whose political sensitivities were keenly developed. Assertions of citizenship are incongruous in a milieu where the governing entity identifies itself with a kingdom, princedom or duchy, or where the conditions of enfeoffment are in force. Increasing appreciation of this issue would suggest to some of the island's population, in particular those among the bourgeoisie who were exposed to current political ideals, that the Grandmaster's wish to be invested with the powers of head of state was not only understandable, but that it could be used as a prelude for their claims to introduce a new political climate in which the Maltese were to have a voice.

At this time, class distinctions were becoming more clearly defined as a result of socio-political and economic developments brought in Malta by the Knights through the introduction of European fashions and new commercial ventures. In the medieval period a middle class was hardly in existence on the island. After 1530 class differences started to become more easily discernible, but it was only in the eighteenth century that the Maltese middle class actively sought greater involvement in politics and governmental issues. In the broader social spectrum, the community of Knights and the local nobility, as well as the higher clergy whose resources and wealth were tied to the tithes accrued from lands, were dominant. Beneath them was placed the bourgeois class, whose fortunes here as elsewhere depended on trade. Peasants and seafarers formed the bulk of society and within this social segment might also be classed the considerable number of artisans and craftsmen, whose prospects may have been somewhat better. Last of all came the beggars and the destitute, whose future was dependent on charity.

The bourgeoisie's claims for greater political power were infrequent in the sixteenth and seventeenth centuries, but there were some voices of dissent. In the 1550s, the medical doctor Matteo Callus was hanged for protesting to King Philip II of Spain about La Valette's despotism. In the seventeenth century, dissent acquired greater political subtlety and procured the support of other powers, as in the case of Don Filippo Borgia, a flamboyant priest from Birkirkara who, hiding under the protection of both the Inquisition and the Church's Curia, wrote a political manifesto against the Hospitaller Order. Absolutism and political arrogance on the part of the Order grew increasingly unacceptable to the Maltese population and gave rise to more frequent protests and some isolated revolts in the late eighteenth century.

These corner balconies were part of the massive alterations affected to the Grandmaster's Palace during Pinto's time.

The response was generally stern and suppression through imprisonment or death was not uncommon.

The Hospitallers' administrative policies arguably reflected those of an ecclesiastical order. The Order increasingly embraced conservatism and grew intransigent and resistant to change, as well as inflexible in its internal structures and reactionary in outlook. The disaffected were distanced and the Order's properties became the reserved asset of an exclusive set, with promotion depending more on corruption and manoeuvring rather than merit, courage or the conduct of an exemplary life.

This decline was to some extent the result of the Convent's struggle to enforce compromise and serenity among the brethren. In fact, the central administration of the Order rarely enjoyed any sustained harmony and it was forced to dedicate time and energy to appeasing antagonisms within its ranks. The lack of unity among the brethren that had been so conspicuous in the early days was again prominent towards the end of the Order's rule in Malta. When the French forces arrived in Malta in 1798, a number of French knights actively sympathised with Napoleon; this was of course a serious act of disloyalty towards the Order. The Hospitaller elites were not ready to mix with the lesser ranking officers. In Malta, such a principle of elitism was not operated, as in Rhodes, through the physical confines imposed by

The pro-Inquisitor and parish priest of Birkirkara, Don Filippo Borgia. Birkirkara Parish Church, Birkirkara.

the *collachio*. Instead, the Knights began to express distinctiveness and aloofness from the rest of the population through the adoption of elaborate ways of address, taking residence in exclusive palatial buildings and wearing gaudy clothes. By the eighteenth century, the religious black habit of the Knights made way for secular outfits tailored in a dandyish style. Meanwhile, the majority of the population lived in small rooms, some even in caves, barely having enough clothes to cover themselves with in winter.

It was inevitable that in such a climate the divide between the governing and the governed would become unbridgeable. The new spirit of the Enlightenment diminished the scope and relevance of the Order, and its ethic began to seem increasingly ill adapted to the times.
In Malta as in Europe, the demand for increased political liberty became more insistent, but the Hospitallers turned a deaf ear. The disregard of the Hospitallers' ruling elite of any delegation of power to the local aspiring politicians and the setting up of a Maltese Langue within the Order were deficiencies that by the late eighteenth century could not be tolerated anymore.

Tsar Paul I of Russia. National Library, Valletta.

In Europe too the Hospitallers' circumstances were distressing. The circumstances of European states acquiring parts of the Order's property either through direct confiscation or by appointing their nominees as bailiffs for the Hospitallers' territories or commanderies were becoming more frequent at the time of Enlightened despots. This was not a time when European states were prepared to tolerate jurisdiction other than their own within their confines.

The decisive moment came with the disappropriation of all ecclesiastical territory in France in 1792. The Common Treasury of the Order was deprived of a major source of its income.
A solution to this financial crisis was again sought in suing for a legacy of territory and the Orthodox Tsar Paul I was approached in the hope of receipt of lands in Catholic Poland. This solution was short-lived as the loss of Malta to the French in 1798 brought this new source of revenue to an end.

On the morning of 9 June 1798, the fleet of Napoleon Bonaparte stopped at Malta on its way to Egypt. Bonaparte requested the Grandmaster's permission to enter the fleet in the harbour but was refused, as according to the international Treaty of Utrecht of 1713, only four ships at a time could harbour in times of war.
Bonaparte took the answer as a personal affront and ordered the invasion of the island. The disembarking French soldiers were faced with little or no opposition as the various garrisons in the massive fortifications surrendered, offering abject or no resistance. The Order suffered the price of internal dissension, as some of its members were unwilling to lend it support. Indeed, when some Maltese militiamen ran to their positions on the forts, they hardly found any weapons.
To make matters worse, a delegation of Maltese nobles and other members of the local elite petitioned the last Grandmaster, the German Ferdinand von Hompesch, for an armistice. The delegation made it clear that the Maltese were generally unwilling to endure an engagement on behalf of an institution that for decades had been unsympathetic to its discontents.
The Grandmaster accepted a truce on 9 June and three days later the capitulation was complete, with the Order signing the agreement by which it ceded Malta to the Republican forces of France.

Epilogue
From Malta to Rome

Grandmaster Ferdinand Von Hompesch (1797-1798). Wignacourt Museum, Rabat.

The aftermath of the loss of Malta was appalling for the Knights. In the following two decades, differences between sections of the Order became more manifest and culminated in the abdication of Grandmaster Hompesch and the creation of a separate faction of the Knights of St John in Russia. Those Knights who at the time of the loss of Malta were at the Russian Court to solicit Tsar Paul I's financial assistance appointed him as their new Grandmaster. The remaining Hospitallers, who were the majority, left Malta with Hompesch for Messina, from where they would later on move to Rome, where they established permanent residence and the Convent. Once again, the donation of money and lands in return for pageantry and honours helped resolve their budget deficit. Married aristocrats and the nouveaux riches in Europe who aspired to knighthood honours began to be more willingly received within the folds of the Order.

In its centuries-old history, the Order's constitution and fortunes experienced many of the tribulations commonly faced by any organisation of note. What sustained it, even when its fortunes were at their lowest ebb, was its entrenchment in a religious ideal. One has to admit, however, that if there is an event that marked forever the future of the Order of Saint John, it is without any doubt the siege of Malta of 1565. In later years its commemoration helped the Order sustain nostalgia for a chivalric past. It is a nostalgia which even now, anachronistic as chivalric ideas may seem to twenty-first century perspectives, plays its part in the Order's survival and its negotiation of the future.

A silver coin showing the face and the coats-of-arms of Grandmaster Hompesch. Wignacourt Museum, Rabat.

Bibliography

Abela, G.F., Della Descrittione di Malta (Malta, 1647).

Balbi di Correggio, F., The Siege of Malta 1565, translated by Henry Alexander Balbi (Copenhagen, 1961).

Bonello, G., 'An Overlooked Eyewitness's Account of the Great Siege', Melitensium Amor Festschrift in honour of Dun Gwann Azzopardi, ed. T. Cortis, T. Freller, L. Bugeja (Malta, 2002) 133-148.

Bono, S., I Corsari Barbareschi (Turin, 1964).

Bosio, G., Dell'Istoria della Sacra et Illustrissima Religione di S. Giovanni Gerosolimitano (Naples, 1684).

Bradford, E., The Great Siege: Malta 1565 (London, 1961).

Braudel, F., The Mediterranean and the Mediterranean World in the Age of Philip II (London, 1986).

Carperntier, J. and Lebrun, F., Histoire de la Mediterranée (Paris, 1998).

Cassola, A., (ed.) The 1565 Ottoman Malta Campaign Register (Malta, 1998).

Cavaliero, R., The Last of the Crusaders (London, 1977).

Skippon, P., 'A Journey tho' part of the Low-Countries, Germany, Italy and France (c.1664-1680)', A Collection of Voyages and Travels, Chruchill, A. .J. (eds), (London, 1732), pp. 618-626.

Ciappara, F., The Roman Inquisition in Enlightened Malta (Malta, 2000).

—, Society and the Inquisition in Early Modern Malta (Malta, 2000).

Coleridge, S.T., The Friend (London, 1844).

The Adventures of Captain Alonso De Contreras, A 17th Century Journey, Translated and Annotated by Philip Dallas (1989).

Doublet, P. J.L.O, Memoires Historique sur l'Invasion et l'Occupation de Malta Par une Armee Francaise en 1798 (Paris 1883).

Earle, P., Corsairs of Malta and Barbary (Malta, 1970).

Galea, M., Grandmaster Jean Levesque de la Cassière 1572-1581 (Malta, 1994).

Grima, J.F., Zmien il-Kavalieri f'Malta 1530-1798 (Malta, 2001).

Hale., J.R., War and Society in Renaissance Europe 1450-1620 (London, 1985).

Hoppen, A., The Fortification of Malta (Edinburgh, 1979).

Mahoney, L., A History of Maltese Architecture from Ancient Times up to 1800 (Malta, 1988).

Maiorano, L., Matteo Perez D'Aleccio Pittore Ufficiale del Grande Assedio di Malta (Italy, 2000).

Mallia Milanes, V., Venice and Hospitaller Malta, 1530-1798. Aspects of a Relationship (Malta, 1992).

—, (ed.), Hospitaller Malta, Studies on Early Modern Malta and the Order of St John of Jerusalem (Malta, 1993).

__, 'Fra Jean de La Valette 1495-1568 - A Reappraisal', The Maltese Cross, T. Cortis ed. (Malta, ca.1995).

Mercieca, S., 'Commerce in Eighteenth-century Malta: The Story of the Prepaud Family', Consolati di Mare and Chambers of Commerce, Proceedings of a Conference held at the Foundation for International Studies (Valletta, 1998), 185-198.

—, 'Le Recit de la Guerre de Troie par Homere et la Chronique du Siege de Malte de 1565 par Francesco Balbi da Correggio: Quelques Observations sur un Heritage Socioculturel Commun', Mediterranées, Revue du Centre d'Etudes Internationales sur la Romanité, No. 29, 2001, 51-62.

—, - 'The Spatial Mobility of Seafarers in the Mediterranean: A case study based on Status Liberi Documentation (1581- 1640)', Journal of Mediterranean Studies, Vol. 12, No. 2, 2002, 385-410.

Muscat, J., The Maltese Gallery (Malta, 1999).

—, The Maltese Vaxell (Malta, 2000).

Nicolai, N. de, Le Navigazioni et Viaggi nella Turchia, Translated by F. Flori de Lilla (Antwerp, 1576)

Quintin d'Autun, J., Insulae Melitae Descriptio (Lyons, 1536).

Riley Smith, J., The Knights of St John in Jerusalem and Cyprus 1050-1310 (London, 1967).

Sandys, G. Travells (1670).

Schermerhorn, E., Malta of the Knights (London, 1929).

Seward, D., Monks of War The Military Religious Orders, (Penguin, 1995).

Sire, H.J.A., The Knights of Malta (London, 1993).

Testa, C., The Life and Times of Grand Master Pinto (Malta, 1989).

Vella, A.P., Storja ta' Malta, Vol. II (Malta, 1979).

Voltaire, Candide (Hachette, 1969).

Wettinger, G., "Early Maltese Popular Attitudes to the Order", Melita Historica, Vol. 6, No. 3, 1974, 255-278.

E-mail:bonechi@bonechi.it

Design and editorial concept: Casa Editirice Bonechi
Graphic design and layout: Serena de Leonardis
Cover design: Sauro Giampaia and *Miller Distributors Limited*

Printed in Italy by Centro Stampa Editoriale Bonechi - *Sesto Fiorentino*

Photographs were taken by Kevin Kasha Photography

ISBN 88-476-1463-5

www.bonechi.com